THE
MEXICAN
COOKBOOK

THE
MEXICAN
COOKBOOK

the practical guide to preparing and cooking delicious Mexican meals

consultant editor
Marlena Spieler

p

This is a Parragon Publishing Book
First published in 2006

Parragon Publishing
Queen Street House
4 Queen Street
Bath BA1 1HE, UK

Copyright © Parragon Books Ltd 2006

ISBN: 1-40548-031-9

Printed in Thailand

Created and produced by
The Bridgewater Book Company Ltd

New photography: Clive Bozzard-Hill
Home economist: Sandra Baddeley
Illustrator: Anna Andrews

NOTES FOR THE READER
This book uses imperial, metric, or US cup
measurements. Follow the same units of measurement
throughout; do not mix imperial and metric. All spoon
measurements are level: teaspoons are assumed to be
5 ml, and tablespoons are assumed to be 15 ml.
Unless otherwise stated, milk is assumed to be whole,
eggs and individual vegetables are medium, and
pepper is freshly ground black pepper.

Recipes using raw or very lightly cooked eggs should
be avoided by infants, the elderly, pregnant women,
convalescents, and anyone suffering from an illness.
Pregnant and breastfeeding women are advised to
avoid eating peanuts and peanut products.

PICTURE ACKNOWLEDGMENTS
The Bridgewater Book Company would like to thank
the following for permission to reproduce copyright
material: Photonica/Getty Images, front cover (top);
Kelly-Mooney Photography/Corbis, page 2, page 5
(left); Macduff Everton/Corbis, page 6 (left); Stuart
Westmorland/Corbis, page 7 (left); Rick Gerharter/
Lonely Planet Images/Getty Images, page 13 (top);
F. Lemmens/zefa/Corbis, page 14 (bottom);
Bob Krist/Corbis, page 17 (top); Danny Lehman,
page 18 (bottom); Envision/Corbis, page 19 (bottom);
Jupiter Images Corporation, page 20, page 21 (top
and bottom); P. Pet/zefa/Corbis, page 24 (top right);
and Gina Martin/National Geographic/Getty Images,
page 25 (right).

Contents

MAIN COURSES

INTRODUCTION

Introduction

Visitors to Mexico are often surprised at just how delicious, fresh, and light Mexican food can be on its home territory. Used to the "combination plates" of Mexican restaurants abroad, they are surprised to discover the delicacy, subtlety, and sheer variety of food in Mexico.

Cocina Mexicana—Mexican food—is the original fusion food. It is a vast collection of cuisines and ways of eating, with dishes that range from simple to blindingly complex. A *taco* in Mexico is in fact one of the country's most modest dishes, simply filled with a few spoonfuls of fire-roasted meat—not ground or pan-fried—and without the usual handful of cheese you find elsewhere. A Mexican meal, too, may have none of the specialties that we tend to associate with Mexican food. Yet always at its heart is the antiquity of the basic ingredients: the many *tortillas*, or flat cakes; *mole* sauce, made of chilies, spices, and chocolate; *salsa*, a spicy sauce made from chilies; as well as whichever beans are special to the region. In fact, take a warm tortilla—the original Mexican cutlery—and wrap it around a piece of your meal—broiled steak, barbecued shrimp, chicken in mole sauce—and presto: you have an instant taco!

Until the "discovery" of the "New World" and the resulting colonization by Spain, the region that is now Mexico was a land of many different tribes, each speaking their own languages and having their own cultures. The Aztec, Mayan, Olmec, Mistec, and Zapotec tribes all had their own way of eating. They were united—to a degree—by the Spanish occupiers, who brought a wealth of new foods, including domestic animals and edible plants such as onions, garlic, and rice. Pigs gave the Mexican table meat, which until then had been very scarce because there were no domestic animals. Pigs also gave abundant quantities of fat for cooking—a new concept for these tribes.

Cows gave milk, which was made into cheeses, and the tradition of cheese-making lives on, with not only the Hispanic cheeses such as *queso fresco*, or fresh cheese, but also with America's Jack cheese, which is said to have originated from Mexican cooks working in California.

Some tribes were more receptive to the foreign foods and influences than others, and certain groups embraced these foods eagerly to improve their quite limited diet, using the fat for pan-frying, the meats for braising and simmering, and the milk for cheeses. The Old World also introduced sugar, which encouraged Mexico's sweet tooth—until then, honey was the only sweetener.

Other Indian tribes adopted many European foods, too, but in a different way. Taken into slavery, they were made to work in the gardens and kitchens of their owners, and the foods they grew and cooked became part of their own diet. All this was part of the huge interchange of foods that accompanied the colonization of the New World. In return, Europe was introduced to chocolate, tomatoes, peppers, and a wealth of foods that transformed both European and Asian cuisines.

The best of Mexican food is an overlay of European foods on top of the ancient pre-Columbian diet of corn, beans, and chilies. The Spanish brought their whole culture, language, and Mediterranean way of eating. Later, the French acquired the colony and brought a tradition of pastry, bread-making, and delicacy, while the Germans, who also had a hand in ruling Mexico before its independence, brought the tradition of brewing beer. Today Mexico is famous for its *cerveza*, or beer, which is refreshing, and perfect with the spicy, south-of-the-border food and the sultry weather.

Mexico is a land of great hospitality. Go to the market and vendors will offer you samples, imploring you to "taste this cactus fruit", or "try this avocado". When you sit down in a restaurant, and especially if you eat in a private home, you will be given food that comes from the heart. It's all so much more than just a plate of food: it is the sum of its parts, its flavor, and aroma, its freshness, its history, and tradition. To eat a Mexican meal is to enter Mexico's culture.

Mexico: A Nation of Regional Cuisines

Mexican food is so regional that it could be considered as a collection of cuisines. Wherever you are eating, the taste of the place is on your plate. There are areas in Mexico where the diet has changed little since pre-Columbian days, yet cities with such a strong European influence that only the tortillas on the table remind you that you are not dining in the Mediterranean.

From the Guatemalan border, where the Mayans once ruled, to the northern reaches of Mexico that straddle and cross over the border into Texas, spreading to the Norte Americano regions of *Chicano* (Mexican-American) culture, each region of Mexican food has its own delicious character.

Some say that Tex-Mex, New Mexican, or Southwestern cuisine cannot truly be regarded as Mexican food, but it can also be argued that these dishes come from areas that once belonged to Mexico/New Spain, or they tend to come from areas with a very large Mexican community. The food is as regional as it is in Mexico, including rice, beans, *masa* (wet flour), and tortillas, yet is based on local, tradional ways of eating.

For instance, *fajitas*, the dish of sizzling beef and onions with flour tortillas, is from the area of northern Mexico/Texas (and is now offered in nearly every Mexican restaurant abroad). In New Mexico you'll find stacked, rather than rolled, *enchiladas* (tortillas in sauce, wrapped around a variety of savory fillings, usually topped with cheese and then baked), which are often topped with an egg. In Arizona, *chimichangas* are flour tortillas that are filled and then deep-fried and/or covered with sauce. And the same style of large flour tortilla in San Francisco has become an entire cult: filled with savory meats, poultry, vegetables, rice, and/or beans, these are known as *burritos* (invented in San Francisco's Mission District, and not, as many people believe, in Mexico).

While the basic foods of Mexico—tortillas, beans, salsa, chilies, rice, and a selection of meats, poultry, fish, and vegetables—remain the nation's everyday meal, it is the type of ingredients and the way they are prepared and eaten that gives the region its personality. And this depends upon the local climate, soil, agriculture, and historical traditions. Will your tortillas be wheat or corn, two-bite delicacies, or huge pancakes able to wrap up a whole meal? What kind of beans will you be eating, and how will they be cooked? Which chilies will enliven your plates, and how is the rice cooked?

Even salsas vary dramatically: some are fiery, made from little more than crushed chilies, while in other areas, salsas are mild and based on tomatoes as well as hot peppers. Some salsas will be flecked with cilantro, while in other areas the herb is not popular.

Tamales, leaf-wrapped dumplings of masa, are a universal Mexican traditional food, with a history of over 4,000 years. The art of the *tamaleria* is a varied one; depending on the region, they are made small or large, empty or filled with sweet or savory mixtures, and wrapped in corn husks in the north or banana leaves in the south.

In the sun- and sea-slashed Baja California peninsula, the diet is all about the fish. Tacos are filled with broiled or pan-fried fish, while fire-roasted lobsters share the plate with refried beans, salsa, and a stack

of warm corn tortillas. In the lush land of Michoacán, everything, including the most delicious strawberries, grows with lavish abandon, and a large lake, Patzcuaro, is famous for its little white fish, served crisply fried and with salsa, of course.

The country's vast coastline offers exquisite fish, from the rustic villages where the fish is seasoned with no more than chili and popped on to the barbecue, to the colonial towns, which specialize in Sunday lunches of *paella* (slow-cooked seafood and/or meat with vegetables and rice), done in Grand European style.

Oaxaca has earned great respect as a culinary center, in part because of its tradition of artisanal chocolate-makers, its seven mole sauces in a rainbow of colors, its inky black beans, and fat tortillas, as well as—for the more adventurous—its crisp grasshopper snacks. And Puebla is home to one of the most famous of all dishes, *Mole Poblano*, a complex sauce of crushed seeds, nuts, dried fruit, tortillas, chilies, and chocolate.

In the Yucatán, where the jungle is dense and domesticated animals are difficult to raise, game—especially venison—is popular. Food is seasoned with seasoning pastes called *recados*, and often meat, poultry, and fish are cooked *pibil*-style, by wrapping the food in banana leaves and roasting it long and slow.

ABOVE **Mexico's vibrant markets and food stalls are a tribute to the wealth of produce that the country has to offer.**

Even Mexico's barren deserts and almost impenetrable jungles offer specialties: is there any land that makes such delicious use of its cactus (*nopales*), cactus fruit, *maguey* (its leaves are used as wrappings for meat), and the agave, which is the basis for Mexico's most famous drink: tequila?

Eating Customs & Food in Daily Life

Mexico is a land of many regions, from desert to tropical jungle to seaside villages and resorts, cities, and countryside, whose mealtimes and eating habits vary greatly. Throughout the country, though, there are about four to five meals in the course of the day, with endless opportunities for nibbling, snacking, eating, and drinking in between.

Breakfast, or *desayuno*, is eaten early, as people rise with the dawn to start their day before the heat takes hold. Mugs of *café con leche* (dark strong coffee with hot creamy milk) are served, as is hot chocolate, Mexican-style—mixed with spices such as cinnamon, cloves, and, sometimes, ground almonds. Sweet rolls go with this, or the best—and classic—accompaniment, *churros*: crisp, golden snakes of airy dough, tossed in sugar. In the countryside, you may be served sweet tamales.

Almuerzo is a second breakfast, what one might call a brunch. It is eaten around 11 am to noon and often consists of robust egg dishes, such as the ever-popular *huevos rancheros* (fried eggs topped with tomato-fresh chili sauce eaten on a fresh corn tortilla). You might find scrambled eggs filling tortillas, splashed with a *pipian* (green pumpkin seed) sauce, or *revuelitos*, scrambled eggs served with either *chorizo* (Mexican pork sausage, rich with spices and chilies) or with tomatoes, cilantro, and chili. Expect café con leche alongside, or switch to a cooling fruit juice or smoothie, with or without milk.

Lunch, or *comida corrida*, is the traditional main meal of the day, eaten around 2 pm; it comprises a relaxed progression of a number of courses, followed by the all-important siesta.

The meal may begin with a few nibbles: *chicharrones* (delicious, crisp pork skin and fat), with salsa to dip into; shellfish cocktail (seafood piled into a sundae dish

LEFT **With Mexicans eating four or five meals a day, and often snacking in between, there are plenty of opportunities to eat out in Mexico.**

and doused with spicy sauce); or oysters with salsa and lime. Or you may be served *guacamole* (avocado, tomato, chilies, and onion mashed with a big squirt of lime); dip into it with *totopos* (tortilla chips), and relax.

The next course is soup: Mexicans love their soups! Richly flavored consommé will be studded with a choice of morsels of meat, vegetables, noodles, crisp tortilla bits, or little round tortilla-dumplings, and accompanied by a bit of salsa and a wedge of lime. Or it might be fish soup instead, or a purée of beans or mashed avocado.

Next comes *sopa seca*. The name literally means "dry soup", but refers to a course of pasta, rice, or tortillas cooked in a casserole (*chilaquiles*). Mexican rice (*arroz Mexicano*) may be yellow in color, tinted and lightly flavored with *achiote* (annato), red from a bit of tomato and/or chili paste, or green with lots of chopped fresh cilantro. Or, it might be multicolored, studded with tiny pieces of vegetables. Mexican pasta is always hearty, often cooked in stock instead of water, with bits of chorizo, vegetables, and often a blanket of melted cheese.

Meat, poultry, or fish comes next, with one or two vegetable dishes alongside: green beans with red bell peppers, *chayote* (a squash-like vegetable) cooked with tomato, or mild green chilies sautéed with onion, for example. There will probably also be a bowl of beans—

pinto, canario, or one of the many regional beans. A stack of warm, fresh tortillas will accompany the meal, with a bowl of freshly made salsa.

As you might imagine, fruit is often the dessert, but Mexicans have a sweet tooth, and sometimes there will be a light dessert such as *crème caramel*—divine with the south-of-the-border influences of coffee, cinnamon, or coconut milk.

Sometime between 6 and 8 pm, you may be offered a sort of afternoon tea without the tea: cups of coffee, chocolate, or *atole* (a warm, sweet drink made from masa) and a tamale or little pastries. Or, you might head into the street instead, for a few two-bite tacos made with the most irresistible grilled meat and tortillas prepared right in front of your eyes, and a bottle of cooling beer alongside it.

Finally, there is *cena*, supper, eaten around 9 or 10 pm, after the day's heat has mellowed, which could be a one-pot dish of spicy, braised meat and vegetables, leftovers from lunch, or a pile of soft tacos, tostadas, *gorditos* (fried, tortilla-shaped masa with a basin for holding a filling), *sopes* (a smallish, fried masa patty), or any of the other savory *antojitos* (tortilla-based morsels). If it is a celebratory occasion, the cena may be taken at a restaurant and be a large, formal meal, lasting until the small hours; otherwise it's a snack, or it may be skipped altogether.

Marketplace & Street Food

In Mexico, eating is an occasion, even if it is only a quick snack bought from a street stall, or a simple meal eaten in a small, family-run restaurant, called a *fonda*. Indeed, street food and marketplace food in Mexico is a revelation of freshness and flavor—the inexpensive simple snack you munch on the spur of the moment may be the most memorable dish you eat on your whole trip.

Walk along almost any street, and aromas waft along the sidewalk where small stands are set up, selling fresh, delicious food of many different types. A whiff of charcoal-grilled meat (*carne asada*) and green onions (*cebollas*) seduces you as you walk by; listen to the patting out of fresh tortillas that will wrap the meat up into soft tacos. A chunk of fish grilled over an open fire is served in a banana leaf, topped with a fresh and feisty salsa, while the lid of a big pan is open to release a fragrant steam—tamales! Just try to refuse: it's impossible to resist.

When corn is in season, it is barbecued on the street, and sold sprinkled with chili powder and rubbed with a little lime juice. Or you might refresh yourself with a chunk of watermelon, orange, cucumber, pineapple, or *jicama*—a crisp, applelike, waterchestnutlike tuber.

Sprinkled with hot pepper and lime, this is zesty and fresh, the heat of the chili brilliantly enhancing the fruity flavors.

A few steps down the street and the whirr of a blender signals that you've reached a *frulatto* stand. Here, orchard and tropical fruits—whatever is in season—are whirled with a bit of sugar and ice, or made creamy with a splash of milk. There may be a wall of glass jars, each with a different colored liquid in it—*aquas frescas* (fresh fruit steeped in sweetened water). Expect to be offered watermelon, tamarind, *limon* (Mexican limes), strawberry, orange, pomegranate, mango—whatever is ripe and in season. A ladle scoops out a cooling mug-full; sip it and savor the essence of fruit refreshment.

Brightly colored scrawled signs on the wall advertise tortas, listing the variety on offer: roasted meat, poached turkey, simmered beef in spicy sauce, chili-spiked chorizo, tangy sardines, grilled beef, braised pork (*carnitas*). A good torta will consist of a hard, chewy roll called a *bolillo*, slathered on one side with hot refried beans, then layered with the meat or poultry of choice, and finished with salsa, avocado, cheese, chopped onions, and/or pickled chilies. Whatever might go into a taco goes deliciously into a torta.

Marketplace food is often Mexican food at its best. For one thing, as with all marketplace food, the raw ingredients are sold right there, so there is little time lost between the purchasing and the cooking. The fondas in the markets are great places to breakfast on hot chocolate and churros, or to take in the later, heartier almuerzo, when the market is bustling. Or stick around and have a nice leisurely comida corrida as the stalls close down and the vendors join the tables for lunch. *Chilaquiles* are one of the most delicious marketplace fonda dishes; made early in the morning, the casserole of corn tortillas, chili sauces, meat/poultry/cheese, and perhaps a few scraps of vegetables grows more tasty as the morning wears on and the dish stays over a low flame. When the tortillas have grown almost porridge-like, chilaquiles are best of all!

Alternatively, the fondas might offer *birria*, a lamb and chili stew; *pozole*, a soup of plump, lime-treated corn called hominy; or *menudo*, a spicy soup-stew of tripe, said to be good for the morning after an over-indulgent night. Or grab a table at an outdoor *cantina* (restaurant) and sample a selection of antojitos or *botanas* (Mexican tapas): sopes, gorditos, *chalupas* (diamond-shaped boats of masa), tostadas, and other delicacies based on crisp masa, topped with all sorts of delicious spicy mixtures.

Visit a park on a Sunday afternoon and you find whole families picnicking, either from packages of homemade food, or from foods sold by vendors scattered

ABOVE **The perfect balance of flavor—Mexican food doesn't come much fresher than the local produce found at the marketplace.**

throughout the parks. In fact, one of Mexico's most famous soups, *caldo Tlalpeno*—a chicken consommé enriched with diced avocado, chickpeas, *chipotle* (a chili), and lime—originated as food sold by a vendor in a park in the Tlalpan district.

In country villages, you'll find women selling enchiladas in big pans often balanced on top of their heads. Get off the bus in a village and chances are that the women of the village will come out and offer their wares—enchiladas that might be no more complicated than tortillas rolled around a thick spicy sauce, but possibly the most delicious ones you'll ever taste.

Special Ingredients

ACHIOTE Small red seeds of the annatto tree. These give a slightly lemony, warm flavor and a golden color to a dish, and in Mexico they are often cooked with rice. Buy already ground into a powder, or buy the whole seeds; soak in a small amount of water overnight, then grind/purée into a paste. Alternatively, you can warm the seeds in oil, then strain and use the golden oil.

BANANA LEAVES The shiny green leaves of the banana plant are used in southern Mexico and the Yucatán for wrapping up tamales and some meats, poultry, and fish for slow roasting. To use banana leaves, heat them briefly over a flame or on a hot grill pan to make them pliable, then carefully wrap them around the filling of choice, using a folding-over motion, as if you were wrapping a present.

CACTUS FRUIT Also called *tuna*, this is a juicy, seed-filled tropical delight, eaten on the streets, peeled, or puréed and strained for ice creams.

CACTUS LEAVES These are known as *nopales*. Cactus is a favorite Mexican vegetable. Often sold whole, with the spikes removed, it has a similar quality to okra, which many people do not like, and a flavor similar to green beans, and can be used in their place in stews and salads.

CHAYOTE A summer, squashlike vegetable, also called *mirliton* and eaten in the Caribbean.

CHEESES Mexican cheeses are different from European cheese in that they are pressed curds and often not aged. They are therefore more susceptible to spoilage, and also do not melt like our traditional cheeses do. Fresh cheese, *queso fresco*, is often used in Mexican cooking; if unavailable, *pecorino fresco*, or fresh ricotta, can be substituted. White cheeses such as Jack, *manchego*, and white Cheddar are great when you're looking for a Mexican melting cheese. And for grating or crumbling, Parmesan, Romano, or dry Jack can all delightfully take the place of *queso anejo*, or aged cheese.

CHICHARRONES Pork skin and fat, often deep-fried to a crisp, puffy state and eaten either as a snack or taco filling.

CILANTRO Fresh cilantro is a pungent, strong-scented herb that is used in many regions of Mexico.

CORN HUSKS Dried husks from ears of corn, these are used to wrap tamales. To use, soak them in warm water until pliable, then smear with a bit of the masa mixture, add a spoonful of the filling of your choice, then close up. Tie with a string or with strands of corn husk.

CORN TORTILLAS A pancakelike flatbread made from specially ground corn. Buy ready-made, or make your own using masa or *masa harina* (dried masa).

CUMIN A lovely, warm and earthy scented spice that is also popular in Middle Eastern and Indian cuisines.

DRIED SHRIMP This is sold whole or ground in Mexican and Asian specialty stores. Used in seafood dishes and in some rice dishes.

EPAZOTE A jagged-edged herb with an oreganolike taste. Add to beans to help mitigate the gassy effect and also enhance their flavor.

JICAMA A crisp, light, giant waterchestnutlike tuber. Eat it raw as a snack or cut it up and add it to salads.

MASA (WET FLOUR) OR MASA HARINA (DRY FLOUR) This is made from *nixtamal*, or ground, lime-treated corn. The lime swells the corn kernels, which then grow out of their skin. They are then ground into a paste and used to make tamales and fresh corn tortillas. Find fresh masa in areas with a large Mexican population, otherwise buy dried masa harina and reconstitute it with water for tortillas or with fat (shortening or vegetable fat) and stock for tamales.

MEXICAN LIMES Limon, a small lemon/lime, is eaten with nearly everything in Mexico; near the Caribbean coast they are small and fragrant. Recipes can use regular limes or lemon in place of these.

PUMPKIN SEEDS (PIPIAN) Buy these shelled in a natural foods store; you can grind them into a paste with spices, or eat whole or toasted.

TOMATILLOS Small, tangy, green tomatoes, covered with a brownish, paperlike husk, which you need to remove before cooking. If unavailable fresh, they can often be found in cans, or you could use gooseberries.

A Guide to Chilies

What sets Cocina Mexicana apart from other world cuisines, and makes it so special, is the array of different types of chilies. Some chilies are so mild as to be eaten as vegetables, while others are so hot that they are treated as condiments to be used sparingly. Dried chilies have a great deal of flavor—some taste of prunes, chocolate, sweet peppers, spices—and are ground into sauces and used for simmering meats, dousing tortillas, enriching soups and stews. They may be sold whole for sauce-making, or powdered to be added in spoonfuls or shakes.

Chilies are an amazingly rich source of vitamins A and C. Their culinary fire is due to the active ingredient 8-methyl-N-vanillin-6-neneamide, also known as capsaicin, and is measured, by a distilling technique, in Scoville units.

Everyone has a different tolerance to a chili's heat. Some can take only a tiny bit while others can eat mouthfuls without a whimper. Eating chilies regularly helps to build up resistance: the more you eat, the easier it is the next time.

When trying to dampen the flames in your mouth, don't reach for water because this just spreads the heat. Carbohydrates such as soft bread, rice, and tortillas help to absorb the irritating substance. Alcohol also reduces the heat. So, if you've bitten off more than you can chew, you've got a good reason to treat yourself to a margarita: the coolness of the ice, and the strength of the alcohol, will help you feel better quite soon. A refreshing cerveza will have the same effect. Yogurt or sour cream (*crema*) are other good heat-relievers: a spoonful helps to soothe the pain.

Always wear rubber gloves when preparing chilies, especially fresh chilies, and never, ever touch your eyes or any other sensitive part of your body with fingers that have touched a hot chili, even long after you were in contact with it. You'll be in pain for hours, possibly days.

FRESH CHILIES Sold green, yellow, and/or red, these may be eaten raw, whether sliced, chopped, or puréed. They may also be eaten roasted and peeled—like any pepper. Whichever way you eat the chilies, you may wish to use a sharp paring knife and remove not only the seeds but also the veins that hold the seeds to the pepper. It is said that these veins, as well as the seeds, are the culprits when it comes to fiery heat! There are three basic types:

SMALL, MEDIUM, TO HOT CHILIES Eaten as a flavoring, an ingredient, or a condiment. Jalapeños are about 2 inches/5 cm long, and about ¾ inch/2 cm wide. *Serranos* are much narrower and slightly shorter. *Gueros* are similar to Hungarian wax peppers.

SMALLISH, VERY HOT CHILIES Also eaten as a flavoring, an ingredient, or a condiment. Cayenne chilies are narrow and up to 3 inches/7½ cm long. They can be green, yellow, or red. *Habañero*, a variety of the Caribbean Scotch Bonnet, is shaped like a spinning top, and is very, very hot with a distinctive, slightly tropical and minty flavor.

LARGE, MILDER CHILIES Eaten as a vegetable as well as a flavoring, ingredient, or condiment. Anaheims are long, light to dark green, and wide enough to be stuffed; they can be mild to medium-hot. *Poblanos* are dark green, almost heart-shaped and shorter than Anaheims; they are perfect for roasting and stuffing. Though usually mild, they can jolt with an unexpected hit of heat.

DRIED CHILIES These are the basis of Mexico's red-hued, many-flavored chili sauces. Except for small, hot, dried chilies such as arbol or cayenne, dried Mexican chilies are mild to medium in heat, and rich with flavor. There are two main types: smooth-skinned and wrinkled. Each has its own distinctive personality and can be used interchangeably: a smooth New Mexico in place of a Colorado or a *chilaca*, for instance, or an *ancho* in place of a *mulatto* or a *pasilla*.

To use whole dried chilies for sauces, you'll want to toast them lightly on a *comal* (a round, flat, cast-iron griddle), taking care not to let them burn. When they lightly smoke in places and change colors from a dark to lighter hue, remove from the heat and place in a bowl. Pour boiling water over them, then cover and let cool. When cooked, the skin peels right away from the flesh and can be puréed into a sauce. (Note: care must be taken when toasting the chilies, as the fumes can irritate the lungs; be sure there is good ventilation and that no one who is suffering from a respiratory disease is nearby.)

PICKLED CHILIES Jalapeños and serranos are both sold *en escabeche* (pickled), sometimes with carrots, cauliflower, and other vegetables. Sometimes small hot chilies, such as cayenne or *arbol*, are pickled in vinegar for a feisty, hot shaking sauce or nibble.

CHILI POWDER This powder (sometimes called mild chili powder) is ground from dried ancho or New Mexico-type chilies, often mixed with other spices such as cumin, oregano, and sometimes paprika. Sometimes it is individual ancho, New Mexico, chipotle, or other chilies; when the powder is made from hot chilies such as cayenne, it is labeled as such.

CHIPOTLE CHILI The smoked, dried jalapeño (and milder Morita) can be sold dried (which you then rehydrate yourself), or it can be sold in a can, preserved in a sweet and spicy, tomatolike *adobo* sauce. This has the distinctive flavor of a barbecue, and is also sold in bottles as a shake-on condiment.

HOT CHILI SAUCES/SALSAS The subcontinent of Mexico is rich with bottled chili sauces—green, red, yellow, chipotle, Tabasco, jalapeño, habañero, and an indefinable number of specialty ones. The only way to decide your favorite is to taste your way through a good selection.

Tortilla Treats, Antojitos, & Botanas: Mexican Tapas

One of the most distinctive aspects of Mexican food is the wide array of dishes based on tortillas, known as antojitos. Antojitos means, literally, "little whims," no doubt because of the variety of toppings that can be added, depending totally upon the whim of the kitchen and also what is available to the cook. These tortilla-based morsels could also be called Mexican tapas, especially when they are very small, or botanas, because of the relaxed way in which they are eaten. In Mexican towns these small, varied platefuls are often cooked on comals by the roadside, and are eaten on-the-go as a tasty and nourishing snack. Here is a brief "cook's tour:"

CAZUELITAS Fried masa, shaped like little pots; similar to *garnachas* and sopes, but deeper so they have a more potlike shape.

CHALUPAS Diamond-shaped boats of masa, about 3 inches/7½ cm long and 1–2 inches/2½–5 cm wide, fried to a crisp, ready for filling.

CHILAQUILES Torn or cut-up, stale tortillas, fried to a crisp, then layered with mild chili or a green tomatillo sauce and another savory ingredient—braised meat, browned chorizo, or shredded chicken—topped with grated cheese and then baked. Chilaquiles are delicious served with fried or scrambled eggs for a supper or morning dish, and leftovers might well find their way into an assortment of nibbles.

ENCHILADAS Tortillas (usually corn) dipped into warm mild chili or green tomatillo sauce, then wrapped around a savory meat, cheese, vegetable, bean, or fish filling. Usually topped with cheese and then baked; sometimes the enchiladas are unfilled, and are simply tortillas dipped into a rich and savory sauce.

FLAUTAS Thin, flutelike shapes, filled with meat or shredded chicken, then rolled up and fried to a crisp; delicious served with guacamole.

GARNACHAS, PICADAS, SOPES OR SOPITAS, THE NAME DEPENDING ON THE REGION A smallish, shallow, cup-shaped, fried masa patty, as thin as possible without tearing.

GORDITOS Fried masa shaped like a small, though thick, tortilla, but with a little basin in the shape, for holding a filling.

HUARACHES An oblong-shaped piece of fried masa, named after the similarly-shaped soles of a type of traditional leather sandles.

NACHOS A layer of tortilla chips or fried crisp tortilla pieces, topped with cheese and salsa, then baked until the cheese is melted. When made well, they are delicious. But even when made badly—as they will be at baseball games, shopping malls, and many chain restaurants north of the border—they can still taste great; it all depends on the cheese and the salsa, and the extra goodies such as beans, sour cream, guacamole, and even chorizo.

QUESADILLAS Tortillas, made from flour, corn, or masa, folded over a portion of cheese, then slapped onto a hot pan. Basically, quesadillas are melted cheese sandwiches made using tortillas instead of bread. In addition to an epazote leaf, which is often used as seasoning, roasted chilies, pickled chilies, beans, braised meats such as carnitas, avocado, seafood, and anything deliciously savory, may be added to quesadillas. Thinly sliced ham is especially good. They are served whole or in appetizer-sized wedges.

TACOS These are made from rolling a corn tortilla around a filling of some sort. For crisp tacos, the corn tortilla is deep-fried until it is as crisp as tortilla chips and just as tasty. Crisp tacos can be filled with shredded chicken, shellfish such as shrimp, spicy and saucy meat, as well as shredded bits of salad, radishes, avocado, sometimes cheese, and/or a little sour cream. By contrast, soft tacos are fresh, warm soft tortillas rolled around almost any sort of filling.

TAQUITOS Tiny, two-bite tacos, which may be either soft or crisp.

TORTAS Hard rolls filled with refried beans (*frijoles refritos*) made from either pinto beans or black beans, depending on the area you are in, and layers of meat or poultry, crumbled or grated cheese, avocado, chorizo, salad, and whatever else the cook has handy. A popular variation of the torta is *molletes*, a torta made with only beans—and sometimes melted cheese.

TOSTADAS A flat, crisp-fried corn tortilla, served topped with a layer of refried beans, simmered or shredded meats, handfuls of lettuce, a crumbling of cheese, perhaps a bit of guacamole, slices of radish, some chopped onion. Tostadas are a great way to use up leftovers in an unusual yet delicious way! Many regions of Mexico have their own traditional tostada recipes: a specialty from the state of Jalisco is tostadas topped with the meat from pig's feet, while in the coastal resort town of Acapulco, tostadas are often topped with crabmeat and avocado with a little sour cream.

Festive Foods

Mexico's celebrations throughout the year are accompanied by special dishes. Mole (see page 174), the sauce of ground nuts, seeds, chilies, spices, and chocolate, which is served with chicken or turkey, was invented by the sisters of a Puebla convent, and is often served for family celebrations of weddings or baptisms, or for Christmas. The classic accompaniment for mole is unfilled tamales.

CINCO DE MAYO "The 5th of May," is the commemoration of victory over the French occupation; it is a festival of Mexican culture, especially popular with Mexican-Americans. Fiestas are held with folk dancing and *mariachi* bands, and specialties such as tacos and carnitas are enjoyed by all.

INDEPENDENCE DAY Held on September 16, this is the biggest fiesta of the year in Mexico, and the streets are full of people celebrating. *Chilies en nogada* (meat-stuffed mild green chilies in walnut sauce with pomegranate seeds) was created for this occasion, because the colors are those on the Mexican flag—red, green, and white.

THE DAY OF THE DEAD November 2 is one of Mexico's most important observations. Families picnic at the cemetery and enjoy bread decorated with sugar crossbones and teardrops, while children nibble on sugar skeletons.

LAS POSADAS Nine days before Christmas, families prepare the *posadas* (nativity crèches), recite the rosary, take part in candlelit processions, and hit the *piñata*— a papier-mâché model of a doll, animal, or cartoon character, filled with exotic candies of mango and chili, lime, and peanut. Each guest is blindfolded and takes a turn to swing at the piñata with a bat. The first one to hit hard enough breaks the piñata and sends the candies tumbling out, with children scampering to gather them up. *Bunuelos* (see page 216), cinnamon-sugar or molasses-coated fritters, may also be enjoyed then.

CHRISTMAS EVE "Buena Noche" is celebrated with tamales (sweet and/or savory) and a sweet, warm drink, atole, made from ground masa and flavored with coconut, strawberry, or vanilla; when made with chocolate, it is called *champurrado*. A gaudy salad is reserved for this evening: lettuce, oranges, beet, bananas, peanuts, rounds of sugarcane, segments of lime, jicama, and pomegranate seeds or small candies.

THREE KINGS' DAY January 6, is a national holiday and is when children receive their Christmas presents. During the day, a sweet bread known as the King's Ring is eaten. It contains a tiny figurine within it, and whoever finds it is obliged to hold a party on February 2, Candlemas Day.

LENT AND EASTER Meatless dishes, such as big, mild chilies stuffed with herby rice, are traditional Lenten fare, while special treats on Easter Day include delicious, marzipanlike candies.

Special Utensils

BLENDER OR FOOD PROCESSOR Sauces are an important part of Mexican cooking, and an electric blender or food processor is useful for quickly puréeing ingredients together.

CAZUELAS AND OLLAS Ceramic casseroles give the special authentic quality of the Mexican kitchen. If you cannot find Mexican casseroles, use Spanish, French Provençal, Greek, Turkish, or other rustic ceramic baking dishes.

COMAL A round, flat, cast-iron grill pan with a handle; any flat heavy pan, either cast-iron or nonstick, is perfect for this pan, which is used for heating tortillas and toasting chilies.

MOLCAJETE AND TEJOLOTE A heavy, stone mortar and pestle, used for the past 3,500 years to grind and purée foods into smooth sauces. In modern days, however, even in Mexico, a blender or food processor is more practical.

METATE A grinder similar to the molcajete and tejolote, though with a large, sloping shape instead of a round shape; metates are for grinding larger amounts of ingredients such as for making mole.

STEAMER FOR TAMALES An ordinary steaming pot, a Chinese steamer, or even a collapsible steaming basket are all great for steaming tamales. If no steamer pot is available, invert a pan in the bottom of a larger pot, just large enough to fit in the bottom of the pan. Fill with enough water to layer and steam the tamales, taking care not to let the pot boil dry, because tamales take a substantial amount of time to steam properly.

TORTILLA PRESS A metal-hinged press used for making corn tortillas. They are usually made out of aluminum or cast-iron, although a homemade tortilla press can be made using wood and hinges. Either way, the masa is rolled into a ball and placed between two pieces of plastic wrap or waxed paper, then put in the flat part of the press. The press is closed and pressed hard to flatten the masa. The masa is removed, the plastic wrap or waxed paper is peeled off, and the tortilla is slapped onto the hot comal.

WOODEN BEAN MASHER Useful for mashing the beans for refried beans; an ordinary potato masher works well instead.

BELOW **Ceramic casserole dishes known as "Cazuelas" or "Ollas."**

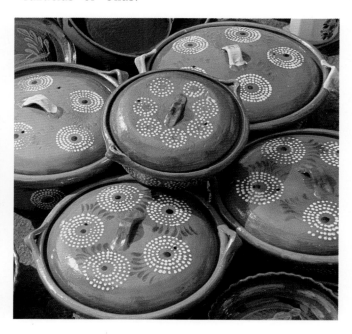

Special Cooking & Preparation Techniques

COOKING RICE To prepare rice Mexican-style, wash and soak the rice for about 30 minutes, then drain and let the rice dry a little or turn it out onto a clean cloth to dry. Heat the oil (the amount called for in the recipe) in a heavy-bottom pan, then turn the rice into it, stirring to coat the rice in the oil, and toast to a nice golden color. Add chopped onion and garlic to cook along with the rice, as well as whatever other flavorings you prefer: tomatoes, roasted chopped bell peppers, corn, chopped carrot and peas, and sliced plantains. This should take about 10 minutes. Add the amount of hot liquid required, stir together, and cook at a slow to medium simmer, covered, for about 10 minutes or until it is nearly done. With the cover on, remove from the heat, and leave to plump up until the rice is tender, for up to 30 minutes.

SHREDDING MEAT FOR PICADILLOS, TACOS, TOSTADAS, AND OTHER SPECIALTIES Traditionally, the meat for tacos and other dishes is simmered, then cooled and shredded by hand or coarsely chopped with a large sharp knife. A delicious and unique dish is *ropa vieja* (old clothing), in which the shredded beef is browned with spices and a little chili sauce, then topped with salad, cilantro, tomatoes, and onions.

COOKING FIDEOS (PASTA) Pasta can be prepared *à la Mexicana* the same way as the rice, with the addition of chorizo, other meats, tomatoes, and a topping of melted cheese.

USING SHORTENING This is the traditional fat of choice in Mexico. Traditional shortening—that is, unhydrogenated—is not only the tastiest choice but also avoids the whole health concern of hydrogenation, which can turn otherwise harmless fats into dangerous trans-fats. Many Mexican stores sell their own homemade shortening, the leftovers of making carnitas (roasted/braised chunks of pork). To make your own carnitas, place about 2 lb 4 oz/1 kg fatty cuts of pork, cut up, in a pan with water to cover. Add an onion, a little cumin, a couple of cloves of garlic, and salt as desired. Bring to a boil and skim off any scum that forms. Transfer all into a baking pan, then place in an oven, preheated to 350°F/180°C, covered, for 2–3 hours. When the meat is tender, remove the cover and let the water evaporate. You'll be left with most of the fat rendered out of the meat. This fat is your shortening; the meat should be cut up into small pieces, and be fork-tender. It is delicious in tacos, quesadillas, or simply on a plate with a stack of tortillas and salsa.

ROASTING AROMATIC VEGETABLES For garlic, place unpeeled cloves on a comal or heavy, unoiled skillet, and cook on each side until the garlic chars. When cooled, the charred skin pulls right away. Onions, often cut into halves, may be cooked in the same way, as can whole chilies, though these may also be grilled instead. Tomatoes, with their juicier nature, may be either charred in the pan and/or under the broiler; the charred skin will peel right off, or it can be ground along with the tomatoes when you prepare the sauce.

TOASTING Many ingredients are toasted/roasted before being added to a sauce—raw tomatoes, garlic, onion, dried herbs, seeds, and chilies are such ingredients. Yucatecan cooks make a whole category of seasoning pastes based on toasted spices and roasted garlic and onion. To toast seeds: in a heavy, unoiled pan, place your seeds—sesame, pumpkin, sunflower— in a shallow layer. Then, over medium heat, let the seeds turn golden, tossing them and turning them often until they do so. Keeping a lid handy is a good idea, as the seeds can pop without warning.

GRATING FRESH TOMATOES FOR A TOMATO PURÉE Cut the edge of a tomato to break through the skin, then grate that cut edge along the large holes of a grater onto a plate; by the time you have finished grating the tomato, you will be left with only the skin. Discard this, and use your fresh raw tomato purée as you desire.

FRYING A SAUCE Sometimes a sauce, especially a mild chili sauce or green tomatillo sauce, will be "fried" after it is puréed. To do this, heat a small amount of fat— several tablespoons—for every generous 1 cup–1½ cups of puréed sauce. Shortening is the fat of choice, though these days healthier oils, such as olive oil and vegetable oils, are also used. When the fat is hot, ladle in the sauce, a little at a time, letting it intensify and reduce, turning from a liquid sauce to a darker, thicker one. Continue until all of the liquid has been added. Taste for seasoning; add a dash of lime or vinegar if needed.

TO THICKEN A SAUCE Thickening a sauce or soup with masa gives a unique and characteristic Mexican flavor. Mix 1–2 tablespoons of masa flour, depending on how much liquid you are thickening, with enough water to make a lumpless paste, then slowly add enough water to make a liquid. Stir it into the hot sauce, and cook, stirring, until it is thickened. If it is not thick enough, add more of this masa mixture. If no masa is available, grind a toasted corn tortilla, or soak one or two in hot water, then purée until they form a smooth, thick mixture. Stir this into the sauce as with the masa.

MAKING TAMALES One of the most unusual of Mexican dishes, Tamales are an ancient food, more than 4,000 years old. They consist of a dumplinglike dough of corn and/or vegetables, wrapped up in leaves —corn husks, banana leaves, or even avocado leaves. The dough may be filled with a spicy meat mixture, or with fish, vegetables, or a bit of chicken or turkey mole. Sometimes an olive is added, or an olive at one end and a few raisins at the other. To make tamales, soak corn husks in hot water for at least 30 minutes, then dry with a towel and fill. Use 2–3 corn husks for each tamale, depending on the size of the husks and the size of the tamales you require. To make a banana-leaf wrapped tamale, prepare the banana leaves by first cutting them into a large rectangle. Then lightly warm them on the top of the stove, turning them over as soon as they lighten in color—taking care they do not burn. As they warm, they will soften and can then be spread with the dough, filled with the chosen ingredients, and folded over in an envelope fashion to encase the filling. After they are filled, steam the tamales until firm—this should take about 40–60 minutes, depending on the size of the tamales.

USING BANANA LEAVES FOR PIBIL Soften the banana leaves as instructed on page 27, then place one or more softened banana leaves on a flat surface so that they overlap. Top with chicken, roast pork, or fish, spiced with a recado, or Yucatecan spice paste. Then wrap the chicken/meat/fish up until it is well sealed. Place in a roasting pan, preferably ceramic, then cover tightly, and bake long and slowly, for several hours. Unwrap, discard the leaves, and enjoy the tender, leaf-moistened and scented meal.

CACTUS PADDLES (LEAVES), ALSO KNOWN AS NOPALES To protect your fingers from spikes, hold the cactus in an area where it has no spikes; use a clean, dry washcloth as extra protection to hold it with. The spikes can be removed simply, using a paring knife to slice away that area of skin and spike, as if you were peeling the cactus. In areas where there are no spikes, you can leave the skin—it has a nice, fresh flavor.

The cactus has a viscous quality not unlike okra, so when using it for salads, salsas, stews, and soups, you'll probably want to blanch it first. Cut it into strips and place in a pan with salted water to cover. Bring to a boil; a thick slimy liquid will emerge. Remove from the heat and rinse the cactus strips. If they are still very slimy, repeat. When they are ready to be eaten, add a little chopped cilantro and onion and proceed as desired. Cactus may also be purchased in a jar or can and is ready to be eaten as it is, without blanching.

PREPARING FRESH PEPPERS AND CHILIES FOR STUFFING On a hot comal or griddle, roast the bell peppers and chilies, such as poblano or anaheim, moving them around, until they are charred evenly; place them in a bowl or plastic bag, and seal tightly. Let steam for at least 30 minutes; when cool enough to handle, peel off the skins, which should have pulled away nicely from the pepper/chili flesh. You may need to use a sharp paring knife to scrape away any stubborn bits of skin. Using your paring knife, remove the inner seeds by cutting a slit in the side and cutting away the seeds inside; if you do it this way, you can keep the stem attached. If you want to avoid the side slit, cut away the stem top and all of the seeds and surrounding matter attached to them. You can then fill the peppers/chilies by filling either the side slit or the top.

PREPARING DRIED CHILIES FOR STUFFING Lightly toast chilies such as anchos and pasillas on a comal or griddle until the color lightens somewhat; you don't want to char the dried chilies as you do the fresh—the sugar content of dried chilies is higher, which means that they burn much more easily. After you have toasted the chilies, place them in a bowl and pour boiling water over them. Cover and let plump up for at least 30 minutes, but up to 2 hours. When they are rehydrated, take the chilies carefully out of the liquid, one by one, and remove the stem and seeds that are attached. Your chilies are now ready for stuffing.

Tortillas

MAKING CORN TORTILLAS

Prepare tortillas using fresh masa (available in some stores in Mexican neighborhoods), or mix masa harina with enough warm water to make a thick paste, thick enough to roll into a ball. Take a generous spoonful, about the size of a double walnut, and press somewhat flat. Place this on a piece of waxed paper or plastic wrap on the bottom half of a tortilla press. Cover with another piece of plastic wrap or waxed paper, then close up the tortilla press, pressing just hard enough to flatten out a round-shaped tortilla. You will get the feeling of exactly how hard to press the more you do it. (Many Mexican home cooks are able to pat out the dough by hand to make tortillas.)

When the dough is the right thickness and flatness, gently peel off the plastic wrap or waxed paper, and place it onto a hot comal or unoiled heavy skillet. Cook over medium-high heat until brown spots appear across the bottom of the tortilla; turn and cook the second side. Place in a cloth-lined basket or on a cloth-lined plate, and close the cloth over the top while you cook the next tortilla to keep it warm and moist. Repeat until all of the masa is used up and you have as many tortillas as you need. Serve wrapped in the cloth at the table so that people can open the cloth, take out a tortilla, and then reclose the cloth, throughout the meal.

To use prepared corn tortillas for making enchiladas, or to wrap around a filling, warm the tortillas one at a time in a lightly oiled, nonstick pan. The warm oil will soften the tortillas and they will wrap easily around your filling.

To heat tortillas to eat on their own or as an accompaniment to a meal, place a stack of corn tortillas on a piece of aluminum and fold it over to encase the tortillas. Heat in the oven or in an ungreased nonstick pan. Another way is to sprinkle each tortilla lightly with water, then place the stack of tortillas in a nonstick pan, and flip the stack every few moments, taking care that the tortilla that is on the outside becomes a tortilla on the inside. Keep flipping the tortillas until they are all warm, then place in a clean cloth and close up lightly. A third way is to cook them one at a time, though if cooking a big batch you will need to keep them warm—Mexicans have special baskets to ensure this, whatever method is used to cook them.

MAKING FLOUR TORTILLAS

Mix 1 lb/450 g sifted all-purpose flour with 2 teaspoons salt and 8 tablespoons shortening or olive oil until it forms crumbs. This can be done in a food processor (if it is too much for your processor, do it in two batches). Slowly work in a generous 1 cup warm water, and blend/knead until it forms a ball of dough—less than 1 minute in the processor, about 3 minutes by hand. Set aside for at least 2 hours to relax the gluten in the flour. Do not chill, or it will be too difficult to roll out. If you wish to do it the day before, refrigerate, but take it out at least 2 hours before you wish to roll it out and cook.

To cook the flour tortillas, heat the comal or unoiled, heavy nonstick skillet to medium. Then take a piece of dough—the size of this piece depends on the size of tortilla you desire. Roll it out on a floured board with a wooden rolling pin until it is paper-thin. A 2-inch/5-cm piece of dough will roll out to about a 7–8-inch/18–20-cm tortilla. Place the dough on the unoiled hot comal/skillet. Leave it for about 20 seconds; if it puffs up, flatten it with the back of a spatula. When brown spots fleck the white dough, turn the tortilla over and cook the second side. Place the cooked tortillas in a clean cloth either on a plate or in a special Mexican tortilla basket. Eat warm or use for burritos, quesadillas, and soft tacos.

Soups & Appetizers

Chicken, Avocado, & Chipotle Soup

 prepare 10 minutes

cook 5 minutes

serves 4

generous 6⅓ cups chicken stock

2–3 garlic cloves,
very finely chopped

1–2 dried chipotle chilies,
cut into very thin strips

1 avocado

lime or lemon juice, for tossing

3–5 scallions, thinly sliced

12–14 oz/350–400 g cooked
chicken breast, torn or cut into
shreds or thin strips

2 tbsp chopped fresh cilantro

TO SERVE

1 lime, cut into wedges

handful of tortilla chips
(optional)

This soup evolved from the foodstalls that line the streets of Tlalpan, a suburb of Mexico City: rich avocado, shreds of chicken, and the smoky hit of chipotle make it special.

1 Pour the stock into a large, heavy-bottom pan with the garlic and chilies and bring to a boil.

2 Meanwhile, cut the avocado in half lengthwise and twist the 2 halves in opposite directions to separate. Stab the pit with the point of a sharp knife and lift out. Carefully peel off the skin, dice the flesh, and toss in lime juice to prevent discoloration.

3 Arrange the scallions, chicken, avocado, and cilantro in the base of 4 soup bowls or in a large serving bowl.

4 Ladle hot stock over and serve with lime wedges and a handful of tortilla chips, if using.

Pozole

prepare 20 minutes
cook 1¾–2¼ hours
serves 4

1 lb/450 g pork for stewing,
  such as lean belly (side pork)
½ small chicken
about 8½ cups water
1 chicken bouillon cube
1 whole garlic bulb, divided into
  cloves but not peeled
1 onion, chopped
2 bay leaves
1 lb/450 g canned or cooked
  hominy or chickpeas
¼–½ tsp ground cumin
salt and pepper

TO SERVE
½ small cabbage,
  thinly shredded
crisp-fried pork skin
dried oregano leaves
dried red bell pepper flakes
lime wedges
tortilla chips (optional)

Hominy (dried, hulled corn) simmered in rich stock is a popular Mexican dish, served with lots of garnishes including tortilla chips, chilies, and lime wedges. If hominy isn't available, you can use chickpeas instead.

1 Place the pork and chicken in a large pan. Add enough water to fill the pan. (Do not worry about having too much stock—it can be used in other dishes, and freezes well.)

2 Bring to a boil, then skim off the scum that rises to the surface. Reduce the heat and add the bouillon cube, garlic, onion, and bay leaves. Let simmer, covered, over medium–low heat for 1½–2 hours, or until the pork and chicken are both tender and cooked through.

3 Using a slotted spoon, remove the pork and chicken from the stock and let cool. When cool enough to handle, remove the chicken flesh from the bones and cut into small pieces. Cut the pork into bite-size pieces. Set aside.

4 Skim the fat off the stock and discard the bay leaves. Add the hominy, cumin, and salt and pepper to taste. Bring to a boil, then reduce the heat and let simmer for 10 minutes.

5 To serve, place a little pork and chicken in soup bowls. Top with cabbage, crisp-fried pork skin, oregano, and red bell pepper flakes, then spoon in the hot soup. Serve with lime wedges and tortilla chips, if using.

Beef & Bean Soup

Stoke up your energy reserves with a bowl of this hearty soup—both comforting and sustaining. It is also highly economical as well as being easy to prepare.

 prepare 20 minutes
cook 35 minutes
serves 4

1 Heat the oil in a large pan over medium heat. Add the onion and garlic and cook, stirring frequently, for 5 minutes, or until softened. Add the bell pepper and carrots and cook for an additional 5 minutes.

2 Meanwhile, drain the beans, reserving the liquid from the can. Place two-thirds of the beans, reserving the remainder, in a food processor or blender with the bean liquid and process until smooth.

3 Place the tomatoes in a heatproof bowl and pour over enough boiling water to cover. Let stand for 1–2 minutes, then remove the tomatoes with a slotted spoon, peel off the skins, and refresh in cold water. Dice the flesh.

4 Add the ground beef to the pan and cook, stirring constantly to break up any lumps, until well browned. Add the spices and cook, stirring, for 2 minutes. Add the cabbage, tomatoes, stock, and puréed beans and season to taste with salt and pepper. Bring to a boil, then reduce the heat, cover, and let simmer for 15 minutes, or until the vegetables are tender.

5 Stir in the reserved beans, cover, and simmer for an additional 5 minutes. Ladle the soup into warmed soup bowls and serve.

2 tbsp vegetable oil
1 large onion,
  very finely chopped
2 garlic cloves,
  very finely chopped
1 green bell pepper,
  seeded and sliced
2 carrots, sliced
14 oz/400 g canned
  black-eyed peas
8 oz/225 g tomatoes
1 cup fresh ground beef
1 tsp ground cumin
1 tsp chili powder
1 tsp paprika
¼ head cabbage, sliced
2½ cups beef stock
salt and pepper

Mexican Fish & Roasted Tomato Soup

prepare 20 minutes

cook 30–60 minutes

serves 4

5 ripe tomatoes

5 garlic cloves, unpeeled

1 lb 2 oz/500 g red snapper, cut into chunks

4 cups fish stock or water mixed with 1–2 fish bouillon cubes

2–3 tbsp olive oil

1 onion, chopped

2 fresh green chilies, such as jalapeño or serrano, seeded and thinly sliced

lime wedges, to serve

Mexico's long shoreline yields an abundance of fish and shellfish, which are often turned into spicy, satisfying soups.

1 Heat an unoiled heavy-bottom skillet. Add the tomatoes and garlic and char over high heat or under a preheated hot broiler. The skins of the vegetables should blacken and the flesh inside should be tender. Alternatively, preheat the oven to 375°F/190°C, place the tomatoes and garlic in a roasting pan, and bake for 40 minutes.

2 Let the tomatoes and garlic cool, then remove the skins and coarsely chop, combining them with any juices from the skillet or roasting pan. Set aside.

3 Poach the fish in the stock in a deep skillet or pan over medium heat until it is just opaque and slightly firm. Remove from the heat and set aside.

4 Heat the oil in a separate deep skillet or pan. Add the onion and cook for 5 minutes, or until softened. Strain in the cooking liquid from the fish, then stir in the tomatoes and garlic.

5 Bring to a boil, then reduce the heat and let simmer for 5 minutes to combine the flavors. Add the chilies.

6 Divide chunks of the poached fish between soup bowls, ladle over the hot soup, and serve with lime wedges for squeezing over the top.

Chilled Avocado & Cilantro Soup

 prepare 15 minutes,
plus 2 hours' chilling

cook no cooking required

serves 4

4 ripe avocados

1 shallot or 2 scallions,
  very finely chopped

3½ cups cold chicken
  or strongly flavored
  vegetable stock

⅔ cup sour cream,
  plus extra to serve

2 tbsp tomato paste

few drops of Tabasco sauce,
  or to taste

juice of 1 lime, or to taste

1 tbsp tequila (optional)

1 tbsp chopped fresh cilantro,
  plus extra to garnish

salt and pepper

4 soft flour tortillas, to serve

The richness of this tasty chilled soup is balanced by the sharp injection of lime and Tabasco. An optional dash of tequila adds an extra kick.

1 Cut the avocados in half lengthwise and twist the 2 halves in opposite directions to separate. Stab the pit with the point of a sharp knife and lift out of the avocado.

2 Peel, then coarsely chop the avocado halves and place in a food processor or blender with the shallot, stock, sour cream, tomato paste, Tabasco, lime juice, tequila, if using, chopped cilantro, and salt and pepper. Process until smooth, then taste and add more Tabasco, lime juice, and salt and pepper if necessary.

3 Transfer the mixture to a large bowl, cover, and let chill in the refrigerator for at least 2 hours, or until thoroughly chilled.

4 Divide the soup between 4 chilled serving bowls and serve, topped with a spoonful of sour cream and garnished with extra cilantro, with tortillas.

Mexican Vegetable Soup

This hearty vegetable soup is found throughout Mexico. Add cheese to melt in, if you wish, and make the soup as hot tasting as you like!

 prepare 10 minutes
cook 40 minutes
serves 4–6

1 Heat the oil in a heavy-bottom sauté pan or pan. Add the onion and garlic and cook for a few minutes until softened, then sprinkle in the cumin and chili powder. Stir in the carrot, potato, tomatoes, zucchini, and cabbage and cook for 2 minutes, stirring the mixture occasionally.

2 Pour in the stock. Cover and cook over medium heat for 20 minutes, or until the vegetables are tender.

3 Add extra water if necessary, then stir in the corn and beans and cook for an additional 5–10 minutes, or until the beans are tender. Season the soup to taste with salt and pepper.

4 Ladle the soup into soup bowls and sprinkle each portion with chopped cilantro. Top with a little salsa.

2 tbsp vegetable or
  virgin olive oil
1 onion, very finely chopped
4 garlic cloves,
  very finely chopped
¼–½ tsp ground cumin
2–3 tsp mild chili powder,
  such as ancho or New Mexico
1 carrot, sliced
1 waxy potato, peeled and diced
12 oz/350 g diced fresh or
  canned tomatoes
1 zucchini, diced
¼ head small cabbage,
  shredded
4 cups vegetable or chicken
  stock or water
corn kernels, cut from
  1 corncob, or 4 oz/115 g
  canned corn
about 10 green or string beans,
  cut into bite-size lengths
salt and pepper
4–6 tbsp chopped fresh cilantro,
  to garnish

TO SERVE
salsa of your choice or chopped
  fresh chili, such as jalapeño
  or serrano, to taste

Spicy-Sweet Meat Empanadas

prepare 15 minutes
cook 15–25 minutes
makes 8

12 oz/350 g ready-made
  puff pastry
all-purpose flour, for dusting
1 egg yolk, beaten with
  1–2 tbsp water

SPICY BEEF FILLING
1 lb 2 oz/500 g fresh ground
  beef
1 onion, very finely chopped
2–3 garlic cloves,
  very finely chopped
¼ cup dry or sweet sherry
pinch of ground cinnamon
pinch of ground cloves
pinch of ground cumin
14 oz/400 g canned chopped
  tomatoes
1–3 tsp sugar
1 tbsp vinegar
3 tbsp chopped fresh cilantro
2–3 tbsp coarsely chopped
  toasted almonds
salt and pepper

TO SERVE
green olives
mixed chilies

This is a great make-ahead appetizer, because it can be frozen for a month and then just popped into the oven at the last moment—it will still taste marvelous!

1 Preheat the oven to 375°F/190°C. To make the filling, brown the meat and onion in a skillet over medium heat. Pour off any extra fat, then add the garlic and sherry and boil down until the liquid has nearly evaporated.

2 Add the cinnamon, cloves, cumin, and salt and pepper to taste. Stir in the tomatoes, sugar, and vinegar and cook over medium heat until the tomatoes have reduced to a thick sauce. Stir in the cilantro and almonds and heat through, then set aside.

3 Roll out the puff pastry into a thin layer on a lightly floured counter. Using a 6-inch/15-cm cutter, cut the pastry into 8 circles. Place a tablespoon or two of the Spicy Beef Filling in the middle of one circle. Brush the edge of the pastry with beaten egg, then fold in half and press the edges together to seal.

4 Press the tines of a fork along the sealed edges of the pastry to make the seal more secure. Prick the top of the empanada with the fork, then place on a baking sheet. Brush with beaten egg. Repeat with the remaining pastry circles and filling.

5 Bake in the preheated oven for 15–25 minutes, or until a light golden brown on the outside and hot in the middle. Serve immediately, hot and sizzling from the oven, with a bowl of olives and chilies.

Seafood Cocktail à la Veracruz

prepare 50 minutes
cook 15 minutes
serves 6

4 cups fish stock
  or water mixed with
  1 fish bouillon cube
2 bay leaves
1 onion, chopped
3–5 garlic cloves, cut into
  big chunks
1 lb 8 oz/675 g mixed raw
  seafood, such as shrimp in
  their shells, scallops, squid
  rings, squid tentacles, etc.
¾ cup tomato ketchup
¼ cup Mexican hot sauce
generous pinch of
  ground cumin
6–8 tbsp chopped fresh cilantro
4 tbsp lime juice,
  plus extra for tossing
1 avocado
salt

"Mariscos!" cry the signs in brightly painted colors along Mexico's beaches and sea fronts, wherever fresh seafood is served. This is a typical salad dish you'll find on offer, full of spicy flavors.

1 Pour the stock into a heavy-bottom pan and add the bay leaves, half the onion, and all the garlic. Bring to a boil, then reduce the heat and let simmer for 10 minutes, or until the onion and garlic are soft.

2 Add the seafood in the order of the amount of cooking time required. Most small pieces of shellfish take a short time to cook, and can be added together. Cook for 1 minute, then remove the pan from the heat. Leave the seafood to finish cooking by standing in the cooling stock.

3 When the stock has cooled, remove the seafood with a slotted spoon. Shell the shrimp and shell any other shellfish. Set the stock aside until required.

4 Combine the ketchup, hot sauce, and cumin in a bowl. Set aside a quarter of this mixture for serving. Add the seafood to the bowl with the remaining onion, cilantro, lime juice, and about 1 cup of the reserved fish stock. Stir carefully and season with salt.

5 Cut the avocado in half lengthwise and twist the 2 halves in opposite directions to separate. Stab the pit with the point of a sharp knife and lift out. Carefully peel off the skin, dice the flesh, and toss gently in lime juice to prevent discoloration. Serve the cocktail in individual bowls with the avocado, and topped with a spoonful of the reserved sauce.

Shrimp & Mango Cocktail

Mango, although lusciously fruity, goes wonderfully well with savory ingredients and is enhanced, not masked, by the robust flavorings. The color of its succulent flesh is an added bonus.

 prepare 15 minutes, plus 2 hours' chilling
cook no cooking required
serves 4

1 Place the tomatoes in a heatproof bowl and pour over enough boiling water to cover. Let stand for 1–2 minutes, then remove the tomatoes with a slotted spoon, peel off the skins, and refresh in cold water. Dice the flesh and place in a large, nonmetallic bowl.

2 Slice the mango lengthwise on either side of the flat central seed. Peel the 2 mango pieces and cut the flesh into chunks. Slice and peel any remaining flesh around the seed, then cut into chunks. Add to the tomatoes with any juice.

3 Add the chili, lime juice, chopped cilantro, and salt and pepper to taste. Cover and let chill in the refrigerator for 2 hours to allow the flavors to develop fully.

4 Remove the dish from the refrigerator. Fold the shrimp gently into the mango mixture and divide between 4 serving dishes. Garnish with chopped cilantro and serve immediately.

6 cherry tomatoes
1 large ripe mango
1 fresh mild green chili, such as poblano, seeded and very finely chopped
juice of 1 lime
1 tbsp chopped fresh cilantro, plus extra to garnish
14 oz/400 g shelled jumbo shrimp, cooked
salt and pepper

Roasted Cheese with Salsa

 prepare 10 minutes
cook 15 minutes
serves 4

8 soft corn tortillas
8 oz/225 g Mexican queso
   Oaxaca, mozzarella,
   or fresh Romano cheese
¾ cup Salsa Cruda,
   or other good salsa
½–1 onion, very finely chopped

The combination of melting cheese and hot salsa is completely irresistible! Called *oueso fundito* in Mexico, it is often prepared on the barbecue to nibble on while you wait for the rest of the meal to cook.

1 Preheat the oven to 400°F/200°C or preheat the broiler to medium. To warm the tortillas ready for serving, heat an unoiled nonstick skillet, add a tortilla, and heat through, sprinkling with a few drops of water as it heats. Wrap in foil or a clean dish towel to keep warm. Repeat with the other tortillas.

2 Cut the cheese into chunks or slabs and then arrange them in a shallow ovenproof dish or in individual dishes.

3 Spoon the salsa over the cheese to cover and place in the preheated oven or under the hot broiler. Cook until the cheese melts and is bubbling, lightly browning in places.

4 Sprinkle with chopped onion to taste and serve with the warmed tortillas for dipping. Serve immediately, because the melted cheese turns stringy when cold and becomes difficult to eat.

SNACKS & SALADS

Chorizo & Cheese Quesadillas

 prepare 15 minutes

cook 30–40 minutes

serves 4

4 oz/115 g mozzarella cheese,
  grated

4 oz/115 g Cheddar cheese,
  grated

8 oz/225 g chorizo sausage,
  outer casing removed, or ham,
  diced

4 scallions, very finely chopped

2 fresh green chilies,
  such as poblano, seeded
  and very finely chopped

8 flour tortillas

salt and pepper

vegetable oil, for brushing

lime wedges, to garnish

The quesadilla is the Mexican take on a toasted cheese sandwich. Oaxacan cheese, also known as Asadero cheese, is the strictly authentic cheese to use, but mozzarella makes a good alternative.

1 Place the cheeses, chorizo, scallions, chilies, and salt and pepper to taste in a bowl and mix together thoroughly.

2 Divide the mixture between 4 flour tortillas, then top with the remaining tortillas.

3 Brush a large, nonstick or heavy-bottom skillet with oil and heat over medium heat. Add 1 quesadilla and cook, pressing it down with a spatula, for 4–5 minutes, or until the underside is crisp and lightly browned. Turn over and cook the other side until the cheese is melting. Remove from the skillet and keep warm. Cook the remaining quesadillas individually.

4 Cut each quesadilla into quarters, arrange on a warmed serving plate, and serve, garnished with lime wedges.

Pork Tostadas

prepare 15 minutes
cook 25 minutes
serves 6–8

1½ tbsp vegetable oil
1 small onion,
  very finely chopped
2 garlic cloves,
  very finely chopped
1 lb/450 g fresh ground pork
2 tsp ground cumin
2 tsp chili powder,
  plus extra to garnish
1 tsp ground cinnamon
6 soft corn tortillas,
  cut into wedges
salt and pepper

TO SERVE
finely diced red bell pepper
shredded iceberg lettuce
sour cream

You'll find this dish throughout Mexico, and across the border in Texas. Replace the ground pork with beef if you prefer and, to save time, use corn chips or nacho chips instead of the pan-fried tortilla wedges (the tostadas).

1 Heat 1 tablespoon of the oil in a heavy-bottom skillet over medium heat. Add the onion and garlic and cook, stirring frequently, for 5 minutes, or until softened. Increase the heat, add the ground pork, and cook, stirring constantly to break up any lumps, until well browned.

2 Add the cumin, chili powder, cinnamon, and salt and pepper to taste and cook, stirring, for 2 minutes. Cover and cook over low heat, stirring occasionally, for 10 minutes.

3 Meanwhile, heat the remaining oil in a nonstick skillet. Add the tortilla wedges, in batches, and cook on both sides until crisp. Drain on paper towels.

4 Transfer the tostadas to a serving plate and top with the pork mixture, followed by the diced bell pepper, lettuce, and a little sour cream. Garnish with a sprinkling of chili powder and serve immediately.

Molletes

Molletes are crusty rolls stuffed with hot beans and melted cheese, then garnished with a tangy hot salsa. In this version, a spicy shredded cabbage salad adds extra crunch to the snacks.

 prepare 15 minutes
cook 20–25 minutes
serves 4

1 Preheat the oven to 400°F/200°C. To make the salad, combine the cabbage with the chilies, olive oil, and vinegar in a bowl. Add the oregano and salt and pepper to taste. Set aside.

2 Cut the rolls in half and remove some of the crumb to make space for the filling. Brush the rolls with vegetable oil. Arrange on a baking sheet and bake in the preheated oven for 10–15 minutes, or until the rolls are crisp and light golden.

3 Meanwhile, place the beans in a pan and heat through with enough water to make a smooth paste.

4 Heat the vegetable oil in a skillet. Add the onion, garlic, and bacon and cook until the bacon is browned and the onion is softened. Add the tomatoes and stir until they have reduced to a thick sauce. Add the warmed beans to the skillet and stir to mix well. Add the cumin to taste. Set aside.

5 Remove the rolls from the oven; keep the oven on. Fill the rolls with the warm bean mixture, then top with the cheese and close up tightly. Return to the baking sheet and heat through in the oven until the cheese melts.

6 Open the rolls up and spoon in a little of the salad. Serve immediately.

4 bread rolls
1 tbsp vegetable oil, plus extra for brushing
2 quantities (or 14 oz/400 g canned) Refried Beans
1 onion, chopped
3 garlic cloves, chopped
3 bacon slices, cut into small pieces, or about 3 oz/85 g chorizo sausage, diced
8 oz/225 g diced fresh or canned tomatoes
¼–½ tsp ground cumin
2¼ cups grated Mexican queso oaxaca or mozzarella cheese

CABBAGE SALAD
¼ head cabbage, thinly sliced
2 tbsp sliced pickled jalapeño chilies
1 tbsp extra virgin olive oil
3 tbsp cider vinegar
¼ tsp dried oregano
salt and pepper

Chicken & Corn Empanadas

prepare 25 minutes
cook 20 minutes
serves 8

14 oz/400 g cooked chicken,
  diced
14 oz/400 g canned creamed-
  style corn kernels
1 small onion,
  very finely chopped
8 pimento-stuffed green olives,
  very finely chopped
2 tbsp very finely chopped
  fresh cilantro
1 tsp Tabasco sauce, or to taste
1 tsp ground cinnamon
12 oz/350 g ready-made puff
  pastry, thawed if frozen
salt and pepper
all-purpose flour, for dusting
beaten egg, for sealing
  and glazing

"Turnovers" do not sound quite so inviting as
"empanadas," but these puff pastry packages are
real winners. They are best eaten when warm,
but their packaging makes them a great portable
lunch or picnic food.

1 Preheat the oven to 400°F/200°C. Place the chicken, corn,
onion, olives, cilantro, Tabasco, cinnamon, and salt and
pepper to taste in a bowl and mix together.

2 Roll out the pastry on a lightly floured counter. Using a
6-inch/15-cm saucer as a guide, cut out 8 circles.

3 Place an equal quantity of filling on 1 half of each pastry
circle. Brush the edge of each circle with beaten egg, fold
the pastry over the filling, and press the edges together to seal.
Crimp the edges with a fork and prick the tops.

4 Place on a baking sheet, brush with beaten egg, and
sprinkle lightly with salt. Bake in the preheated oven for 20
minutes, or until golden brown and piping hot in the center.

Tamales

 prepare 30 minutes,
plus 3 hours' soaking
cook 40–60 minutes
serves 4–6

8–10 corn husks or several
  banana leaves, cut into
  12-inch/30-cm squares
6 tbsp shortening or white
  vegetable fat
½ tsp salt
pinch of sugar
pinch of ground cumin
scant 1⅝ cups masa harina
½ tsp baking powder
about 1 cup beef, chicken,
  or vegetable stock

FILLING
½ cup cooked corn kernels,
  mixed with a little grated
  cheese and chopped fresh
  green chili (such as poblano
  or serrano), or pork simmered
  in a mild chili sauce

TO SERVE
shredded lettuce, such as
  romaine or iceberg
tomato wedges
salsa of your choice

Traditional Mexican fare, tamales are large
dumplings of corn flour, stuffed with a moist
filling, then wrapped in either banana leaves or
corn husks. They make attractive party food.

1 If using corn husks, soak in enough hot water to cover for
at least 3 hours or overnight. If using banana leaves, warm
them by placing over an open flame for just a few seconds, to
make them pliable.

2 To make the tamale dough, beat the shortening until fluffy
in a bowl, then beat in the salt, sugar, cumin, masa harina,
and baking powder until the mixture resembles very
fine crumbs.

3 Add the stock very gradually, in several batches, beating
until the mixture becomes fluffy and resembles
whipped cream.

4 Spread 1–2 tablespoons of the tamale mixture on either a
soaked and drained corn husk or a piece of pliable heated
banana leaf.

5 Spoon in the filling. Fold the sides of the husks or leaves
over the filling to enclose. Wrap each package in a square
of foil and arrange in a steamer.

6 Pour enough hot water into the bottom of the steamer,
cover, and boil. Steam for 40–60 minutes, topping up the
water in the bottom of the steamer when needed. Remove
the tamales, unwrap, and serve with shredded lettuce, tomato
wedges, and salsa.

Huevos Rancheros

Spice up your morning with these ranch-style or country-style eggs—an ideal dish for a weekend brunch. You can reduce the number of chilies if it's too early in the morning for a fiery hit.

 prepare 15 minutes
cook 35–40 minutes
serves 4

1 Heat the butter in a heavy-bottom skillet over medium heat. Add the onions and garlic and cook, stirring frequently, for 5 minutes, or until softened. Add the bell peppers and chilies and cook for 5 minutes, or until softened.

2 Place the tomatoes in a heatproof bowl and pour over enough boiling water to cover. Let stand for 1–2 minutes, then remove the tomatoes with a slotted spoon, peel off the skins, and refresh in cold water. Chop the flesh.

3 Preheat the oven to 350°F/180°C. Add the tomatoes, lemon juice, and oregano and season to taste with salt and pepper. Bring to a boil, then reduce the heat, cover, and let simmer for 10 minutes, or until thickened, adding a little more lemon juice if the mixture becomes too dry.

4 Transfer the mixture to a large, ovenproof dish. Make 4 hollows in the mixture and break an egg into each. Bake in the preheated oven for 12–15 minutes, or until the eggs are set.

5 Sprinkle with grated cheese and return to the oven for 3–4 minutes, or until the cheese has melted. Serve immediately with flour tortillas.

2 tbsp butter, bacon fat,
  or shortening
2 onions, very finely chopped
2 garlic cloves,
  very finely chopped
2 red or yellow bell peppers,
  seeded and diced
2 fresh mild green chilies,
  such as poblano, seeded
  and very finely chopped
4 large ripe tomatoes
2 tbsp lemon or lime juice
2 tsp dried oregano
4 large eggs
3 oz/85 g Cheddar cheese,
  grated
salt and pepper
4 soft flour tortillas, to serve

Nachos

prepare 10 minutes

cook 5–8 minutes

serves 6

2 quantities (or 14 oz/400 g canned) Refried Beans

6 oz/175 g tortilla chips

2 tbsp very finely chopped bottled jalapeño chilies

7 oz/200 g canned or bottled pimentos or roasted bell peppers, drained and finely sliced

4 oz/115 g Gruyère cheese, grated

4 oz/115 g Cheddar cheese, grated

salt and pepper

Who can resist diving into a molten mountain of nachos and biting into that great combination of the soggy, chewy, and crispy? Nachos are so easy to prepare, especially if you use canned refried beans.

1 Preheat the oven to 400°F/200°C. Place the Refried Beans in a pan with a tiny amount of water and then heat through gently.

2 Spread the tortilla chips out over the bottom of a large, shallow, ovenproof dish or roasting pan. Cover with the warmed Refried Beans. Sprinkle over the chilies and pimentos and season to taste with salt and pepper. Mix the cheeses together in a bowl and sprinkle on top.

3 Bake in the preheated oven for 5–8 minutes, or until the cheese is bubbling and melted. Serve immediately.

Black Bean Nachos

 prepare 15 minutes, plus
8 hours' soaking (optional)
cook 1¾ hours
serves 4

1⅓ cups dried black beans, or
  canned black beans, drained
1½–2 cups grated cheese, such
  as Cheddar, fontina, Romano,
  Asiago, or a combination
about ¼ tsp cumin seeds
  or ground cumin
about 4 tbsp sour cream
thinly sliced pickled jalapeño
  chilies (optional)
1 tbsp chopped fresh cilantro
handful of shredded lettuce,
  such as romaine or iceberg
tortilla chips, to serve

Packed with Mexican flavors, this tasty black bean and cheese dip is fun to eat and will get any meal off to a good start!

1 If using dried black beans, soak them overnight, then drain. Put in a pan, cover with water, and bring to a boil. Boil for 10 minutes, then reduce the heat and let simmer for 1½ hours, or until tender. Drain well.

2 Preheat the oven to 375°F/190°C. Spread the beans in a shallow ovenproof dish, then sprinkle the cheese over the top. Sprinkle with cumin to taste.

3 Bake in the preheated oven for 10–15 minutes, or until the beans are cooked through and the cheese is bubbly and melted.

4 Remove from the oven and spoon the sour cream on top. Add the chilies, if using, and sprinkle with cilantro and lettuce.

5 Arrange the tortilla chips around the beans, placing them in the mixture. Serve the nachos immediately.

Tortas

Throughout Mexico you'll find street vendors selling these substantial Mexican rolls. Filled with all sorts of ingredients, they are "Muy Delicioso!" Make your own and vary the filling as you wish.

 prepare 10 minutes
cook 10 minutes
serves 4

1 Cut the rolls in half and remove a little of the crumb to make space for the filling.

2 Brush the outside and inside of the rolls with butter and toast, on both sides, on a hot griddle or in a skillet for a few minutes until crisp. Alternatively, preheat the oven to 400°F/200°C and bake until lightly toasted.

3 Meanwhile, place the beans in a pan with a tiny amount of water and heat through gently.

4 Cut the avocado in half lengthwise and twist the 2 halves in opposite directions to separate. Stab the pit with the point of a sharp knife and lift out. Carefully peel off the skin, dice the flesh, and toss in lime juice to prevent discoloration.

5 When the rolls are heated, spread one half of each roll generously with the beans, then top with a layer of cooked meat. Top with tomato, onion, cilantro, and the avocado.

6 Generously spread sour cream onto the other side of each roll. Drizzle the salsa over the filling, add a little shredded lettuce, then sandwich the two sides of each roll together; press tightly. Serve immediately.

4 crusty rolls, such as French rolls or bocadillos
melted butter or olive oil, for brushing
1 quantity (or 8 oz/225 g canned) Refried Beans
1 avocado
lime juice, for tossing
12 oz/350 g shredded cooked chicken, browned chorizo sausage pieces, sliced ham and cheese, or any leftover cooked meat you have to hand
1 ripe tomato, sliced or diced
1 small onion, very finely chopped
2 tbsp chopped fresh cilantro
4–6 tbsp sour cream or strained plain yogurt
salsa of your choice
handful of shredded lettuce, such as romaine or iceberg

Steak, Avocado, & Bean Salad

 prepare 15 minutes,
plus 30 minutes' marinating
cook 6 minutes
serves 4

12 oz/350 g tender steak, such
   as sirloin or tenderloin
4 garlic cloves, chopped
juice of 1 lime, plus extra
   for tossing
4 tbsp extra virgin olive oil
1 tbsp wine vinegar
¼ tsp mild chili powder,
   such as ancho or New Mexico
¼ tsp ground cumin
½ tsp paprika
pinch of sugar (optional)
1 avocado
5 scallions, thinly sliced
about 7 oz/200 g crisp lettuce
   leaves, such as romaine, or
   mixed fresh herb leaves
8 oz/225 g canned corn kernels,
   drained
14 oz/400 g canned pinto, black,
   or red kidney beans, drained
2 ripe tomatoes, diced
¼ fresh green or red chili,
   such as poblano or Anaheim,
   chopped
3 tbsp chopped fresh cilantro
handful of crisp tortilla chips,
   broken into pieces
salt and pepper

The Californian influence on Mexican food is evident in this big, hearty salad. Packed with delicious ingredients, this fantastic dish is a meal in itself.

1 Place the steak in a nonmetallic dish with the garlic and half the lime juice and oil. Season to taste with salt and pepper, cover, and let marinate for 30 minutes.

2 To make the dressing, combine half the lime juice and half the oil with the vinegar, chili powder, cumin, and paprika in a small nonmetallic bowl. Add the sugar, if using, then set aside.

3 Pan-fry the steak, or cook under a hot broiler, until browned on the outside and cooked to your liking in the middle. Remove from the skillet or broiler, cut into strips, and set aside; keep warm or let cool.

4 Cut the avocado in half lengthwise and twist the 2 halves in opposite directions to separate. Stab the pit with the point of a sharp knife and lift out. Carefully peel off the skin, dice the flesh, and toss in lime juice to prevent discoloration.

5 Toss the scallions with the lettuce and arrange on a serving plate. Pour half the dressing over the leaves, then arrange the corn, beans, avocado, and tomatoes over the top. Sprinkle with the chili and cilantro.

6 Arrange the steak and the tortilla chips on top, pour over the rest of the dressing, and serve immediately.

Ceviche Salad

 prepare 20 minutes,
plus 8 hours' chilling

cook no cooking required

serves 4

1 lb/450 g salmon, red snapper,
  or sole fillets, skinned and cut
  into strips or slices
1 small onion,
  very finely chopped
1 fresh jalapeño chili or
  2 small fresh mild green
  chilies, such as poblano,
  seeded and very finely
  chopped
juice of 3 limes
1 tbsp extra virgin olive oil
1 tbsp chopped fresh cilantro,
  plus extra to garnish
1 tbsp snipped fresh chives or
  dill
2 tomatoes
1 ripe avocado
2 tbsp capers, rinsed (optional)
salt and pepper

This elegant appetizer couldn't be simpler to make but requires several hours' chilling for the raw fish to "cook" in the lime juice—you can tell that it's done when the strips of fish turn opaque.

1 Place the fish, onion, chili, lime juice, oil, and herbs in a nonmetallic dish and mix together. Cover and let chill in the refrigerator for 8 hours or overnight, stirring occasionally to ensure that the fish is well coated in the marinade.

2 When ready to serve, remove the dish from the refrigerator and season to taste with salt and pepper.

3 Place the tomatoes in a heatproof bowl and pour over boiling water to cover. Let stand for 1–2 minutes, then remove the tomatoes with a slotted spoon. Peel and then cut the flesh into thin slices.

4 Cut the avocado in half lengthwise and twist the 2 halves in opposite directions to separate. Stab the pit with the point of a sharp knife and lift out. Peel off the skin, then cut the flesh into thin slices.

5 Arrange the fish mixture on a serving plate with the tomatoes and avocado, then sprinkle with the capers, if using. Sprinkle with chopped cilantro to garnish.

Note People with certain diseases (such as diabetes or liver disease) or weakened immune systems should never eat raw fish. The elderly and pregnant women (along with breastfeeding mothers and infants) should also avoid eating raw fish.

Zucchini with Green Chili Vinaigrette

Lightly cooked zucchini are mixed with ripe, juicy tomatoes and dressed with a chili vinaigrette to create a perfect side salad for a summer lunch or supper.

 prepare 30 minutes
cook 10 minutes,
plus 20 minutes' standing
serves 4

1 Roast the chili, or the combination of the green bell pepper and chili, in a unoiled heavy-bottom skillet or under a preheated hot broiler until the skin is charred. Place in a plastic bag, twist to seal well, and let stand for 20 minutes.

2 Peel the skin from the chili and bell pepper, if using, then remove the seeds and slice the flesh. Set aside.

3 Bring about 2 inches/5 cm of water to a boil in the bottom of a steamer. Add the zucchini to the top part of the steamer, cover, and steam for 5 minutes, or until just tender.

4 Meanwhile, thoroughly combine the dressing ingredients in a bowl. Stir in the chili, and bell pepper if using, then season to taste with salt and pepper.

5 Arrange the zucchini and tomatoes in a serving bowl or on a platter and spoon over the chili dressing. Toss gently and serve with tortilla chips, if wished.

1 large fresh mild green chili,
  such as poblano, or a
  combination of 1 green
  bell pepper and ½–1 fresh
  green chili
4 zucchini, sliced
4 ripe tomatoes, diced or sliced
salt and pepper
tortilla chips, to serve (optional)

DRESSING
2–3 garlic cloves,
  very finely chopped
pinch of sugar
¼ tsp ground cumin
2 tbsp white wine vinegar
4 tbsp extra virgin olive oil
2–3 tbsp chopped fresh cilantro

Papaya, Avocado, & Red Bell Pepper Salad

 prepare 20 minutes

cook no cooking required

serves 4–6

7 oz/200 g mixed green
  salad leaves
2–3 scallions, chopped
3–4 tbsp chopped fresh cilantro
1 small papaya
2 red bell peppers,
  seeded and thinly sliced
1 avocado
lime juice, for tossing
3–4 tbsp pumpkin seeds
  (pepitas), preferably toasted
  (optional)

DRESSING
juice of 1 lime
large pinch of paprika
large pinch of ground cumin
large pinch of sugar
1 garlic clove,
  very finely chopped
4 tbsp extra virgin olive oil
salt
dash of white wine vinegar
  (optional)

This colorful and refreshing salad, with its sweet and spicy flavors, is the perfect foil to a meaty main dish, and is particularly good with barbecued food.

1 Combine the salad leaves with the scallions and cilantro in a bowl. Mix well, then transfer the salad to a large serving dish.

2 Cut the papaya in half and scoop out the seeds with a spoon. Cut into quarters, remove the peel, and slice the flesh. Arrange on top of the salad leaves, and add the bell peppers.

3 Cut the avocado in half lengthwise and twist the 2 halves in opposite directions to separate. Stab the pit with the point of a sharp knife and lift out. Carefully peel off the skin, dice the flesh, and toss in lime juice to prevent discoloration. Add to the other salad ingredients.

4 To make the dressing, whisk the lime juice, paprika, cumin, sugar, garlic, and oil together in a small bowl. Season to taste with salt.

5 Pour the dressing over the salad and toss lightly, adding a dash of wine vinegar if a flavor with more "bite" is preferred. Sprinkle with pumpkin seeds (pepitas), if using.

Citrus Salad with Pomegranate

prepare 20 minutes

cook no cooking required

serves 4

A salad like this reveals how much Mexico and the Mediterranean share in terms of sunny flavors and ingredients.

1 large pomegranate
1 grapefruit
2 sweet oranges
finely grated rind of ½ lime
1–2 garlic cloves,
   very finely chopped
3 tbsp red wine vinegar
juice of 2 limes
½ tsp sugar
¼ tsp dry mustard
4–5 tbsp extra virgin olive oil
1 avocado
lime or lemon juice,
   for tossing
1 head red leafy lettuce,
   such as oak leaf
salt and pepper
½ red onion, thinly sliced,
   to garnish

1 Cut the pomegranate into quarters, then press back the outer skin to push out the seeds into a bowl.

2 Using a sharp knife, cut a slice off the top and bottom of the grapefruit, then remove the peel and pith, cutting downward. Cut out the segments from between the membranes, then add to the pomegranate.

3 Finely grate the rind of half an orange and set aside. Using a sharp knife, cut a slice off the top and bottom of both oranges, then remove the peel and pith, cutting downward and taking care to retain the shape of the oranges. Slice horizontally into slices, then cut into quarters. Add the oranges to the pomegranate and grapefruit and stir to mix well.

4 Combine the orange rind with the lime rind, garlic, vinegar, lime juice, sugar, and mustard in a nonmetallic bowl. Season to taste, then whisk in the oil.

5 Cut the avocado in half lengthwise and twist the 2 halves in opposite directions to separate. Stab the pit with the point of a sharp knife and lift out. Carefully peel off the skin, dice the flesh, and toss in lime juice to prevent discoloration.

6 Place the lettuce in a serving bowl. Top with the fruit and avocado, then pour over the dressing and toss. Garnish with the onion and serve immediately.

MAIN COURSES

Tequila-Marinated Beef Steaks

 prepare 10 minutes,
plus 2 hours' marinating
and 30 minutes' standing
cook 6–8 minutes
serves 4

4 sirloin steaks
salt and pepper

MARINADE
2 tbsp olive oil
3 tbsp tequila
3 tbsp orange juice
1 tbsp lime juice
3 garlic cloves, crushed
2 tsp mild chili powder,
  such as ancho or New Mexico
2 tsp ground cumin
1 tsp dried oregano

TO SERVE
corn and red pepper salsa
potato slices or chunks

Now it's barbecue time, Mexican style, with a marinade guaranteed to make your meat melt in the mouth. If the weather is looking less than favorable, cook the steaks under a preheated hot broiler.

1 To make the marinade, place all the ingredients, plus salt and pepper to taste, in a large, shallow, nonmetallic dish and mix together. Add the steaks and turn to coat in the marinade. Cover and let chill in the refrigerator for at least 2 hours or overnight, turning occasionally.

2 Preheat the barbecue and oil the grill rack. Let the steaks return to room temperature for 30 minutes, then remove from the marinade. Cook over hot coals for 3–4 minutes on each side for medium, or longer according to taste, basting frequently with the remaining marinade. Serve immediately.

Chilies Stuffed with Beef

 prepare 15 minutes,
plus 20 minutes' standing
cook 30–40 minutes
serves 4

4 large fresh poblano chilies
all-purpose flour, for dusting
vegetable oil, for cooking

SPICY BEEF FILLING
1 lb 2 oz/500 g fresh
  ground beef
1 onion, very finely chopped
2–3 garlic cloves,
  very finely chopped
¼ cup dry or sweet sherry
pinch of ground cinnamon
pinch of ground cloves
pinch of ground cumin
14 oz/400 g canned
  chopped tomatoes
1–3 tsp sugar
1 tbsp vinegar
3 tbsp chopped fresh cilantro
2–3 tbsp coarsely chopped
  toasted almonds
salt and pepper

BATTER
3 eggs, separated
6–8 tbsp all-purpose flour
pinch of salt
about ½ cup water
Quick Tomato Sauce, to serve

Large, mildish-tasting green chilies are roasted, peeled, and stuffed with a succulent meat mixture that is sweet, spicy, and punctuated with nuts.

1 Roast the chilies in an unoiled skillet or under a preheated broiler until the skin is charred. Place in a plastic bag, twist to seal and let stand for 20 minutes. Make a slit in the side of each chili and remove the seeds, leaving the stems intact. Set aside.

2 To make the filling, brown the ground beef and onion in a heavy-bottom skillet over medium heat. Pour off any extra fat, then add the garlic and sherry and boil down until the liquid has nearly evaporated.

3 Add the cinnamon, cloves, cumin, and salt and pepper to taste. Stir in the tomatoes, sugar, and vinegar and cook over medium heat until the tomatoes have reduced to a thick sauce.

4 Stir in the cilantro and almonds and heat through. Stuff as much of the filling into the chilies as will fit, then dust each with flour. Set aside.

5 To make the batter, in a large bowl, beat the yolks with the flour, salt, and enough of the water to make a thick mixture. In a separate bowl, whisk the egg whites until they form stiff peaks. Fold the egg whites into the batter, then dip each chili into the batter.

6 Heat the oil in a deep skillet until very hot and just smoking. Add the chilies and cook until they are golden brown. Serve hot, with the tomato sauce.

Chili con Carne

This is a modern variation on the classic chili, with chunks of beef rather than ground meat and without beans. The chocolate gives extra depth to the sauce.

prepare 15 minutes

cook 2½–3½ hours

serves 4

1 Dry-fry the cumin seeds in a heavy-bottom skillet over medium heat, shaking the skillet, for 3–4 minutes, or until lightly toasted. Let cool, then grind in a mortar with a pestle. Alternatively, use a coffee grinder reserved for the purpose.

2 Toss the beef in the seasoned flour to coat. Melt the fat in a large, heavy-bottom pan. Add the beef, in batches, and cook until browned on all sides. Remove the beef with a slotted spoon and set aside.

3 Add the onions and garlic to the pan and cook gently for 5 minutes, or until softened. Add the cumin, oregano, paprika, and chilies and cook, stirring, for 2 minutes. Return the beef to the pan, pour over the lager, then add the chocolate. Bring to a boil, stirring, then reduce the heat, cover, and let simmer for 2–3 hours, or until the beef is very tender, adding more lager if necessary.

1 tbsp cumin seeds

1 lb 7 oz/650 g top round,
cut into 1-inch/2.5-cm cubes

all-purpose flour, well seasoned
with salt and pepper,
for coating

3 tbsp beef drippings, bacon fat,
or vegetable oil

2 onions, very finely chopped

4 garlic cloves,
very finely chopped

1 tbsp dried oregano

2 tsp paprika

4 dried red chilies, such as
ancho or pasilla, crushed,
or to taste

1 large bottle of South
American lager

4 oz/115 g semisweet chocolate

Ropa Vieja

 prepare 15 minutes,
plus 30 minutes' cooling

cook 2¼ hours

serves 6

3 lb 5 oz/1.5 kg flank beef steak
  or other stewing meat
beef stock
1 carrot, sliced
10 garlic cloves, sliced
2 tbsp vegetable oil
2 onions, thinly sliced
3–4 mild fresh green chilies,
  such as poblano, seeded
  and sliced
salt and pepper
warmed flour tortillas, to serve

SALAD GARNISHES
3 ripe tomatoes, diced
8–10 radishes, diced
3–4 tbsp chopped fresh cilantro
4–5 scallions, chopped
1–2 limes, cut into wedges

Fill warmed tortillas with this tender, browned beef and a selection of crisp vegetables to make wonderful tacos.

1 Place the meat in a large pan and cover with a mixture of stock and water. Add the carrot and half the garlic with salt and pepper to taste. Cover and bring to a boil, then reduce the heat to low. Skim the scum that rises to the surface, then re-cover the pan and cook the meat gently for 2 hours, or until very tender.

2 Remove the pan from the heat and let the meat cool in the liquid. When cool enough to handle, remove from the liquid and shred with your fingers and a fork.

3 Heat the oil in a large, heavy-bottom skillet. Add the remaining garlic, the onions, and chilies and cook until lightly colored. Remove from the skillet and set aside.

4 Add the meat to the skillet and cook over medium–high heat until browned and crisp. Transfer to a serving dish. Top with the onion mixture and surround with the tomatoes, radishes, cilantro, scallions, and lime wedges. Serve with warmed tortillas.

Beef Enchiladas

prepare 15 minutes

cook 1 hour

serves 4

2 tbsp olive oil,
  plus extra for oiling
2 large onions, thinly sliced
1 lb 4 oz/550 g lean beef,
  cut into bite-size pieces
1 tbsp ground cumin
1–2 tsp cayenne pepper,
  or to taste
1 tsp paprika
8 soft corn tortillas
8 oz/225 g Cheddar cheese,
  grated
salt and pepper

TACO SAUCE

1 tbsp olive oil
1 onion, very finely chopped
1 green bell pepper,
  seeded and diced
1–2 fresh hot green chilies,
  such as jalapeño, seeded
  and very finely chopped
3 garlic cloves, crushed
1 tsp ground cumin
1 tsp ground coriander
1 tsp brown sugar
1 lb/450 g ripe tomatoes,
  peeled and coarsely chopped
juice of ½ lemon
salt and pepper

This is a dish for those seriously committed to comfort eating. It would be equally effective with good-quality ground beef in place of the pieces of beef, if you prefer.

1 Preheat the oven to 350°F/180°C. Oil a large, rectangular baking dish.

2 To make the sauce, heat the oil in a deep skillet over medium heat. Add the onion and cook for 5 minutes, or until softened. Add the bell pepper and chilies and cook for 5 minutes. Add the garlic, cumin, coriander, and sugar and cook the sauce for an additional 2 minutes, stirring. Add the tomatoes, lemon juice, and salt and pepper to taste. Bring to a boil, then reduce the heat and let simmer for 10 minutes.

3 Meanwhile, heat the oil in a large skillet over low heat. Add the onions and cook for 10 minutes, or until soft. Remove with a slotted spoon and set aside.

4 Increase the heat to high, add the beef, and cook, stirring, for 2–3 minutes, or until browned on all sides. Reduce the heat to medium, add the spices and salt and pepper to taste, and cook, stirring constantly, for 2 minutes.

5 Warm each tortilla in a lightly oiled nonstick skillet for 15 seconds on each side, then dip each, in turn, in the sauce. Top with a little of the beef, onions, and grated cheese and roll up. Place seam-side down in the prepared baking dish, top with the remaining sauce and grated cheese, and bake in the preheated oven for 30 minutes. Serve immediately.

Michoacán Beef

This rich, smoky-flavored stew is delicious; leftovers make a great filling for tacos, too!

 prepare 10 minutes
cook 2 hours
serves 4–6

1 If you are using dried chipotle chilies, place them in a pan with enough water to cover. Protecting your face against fumes and making sure that the kitchen is well ventilated, bring the chilies and water to a boil. Cook for 5 minutes, then remove the pan from the heat, cover, and let stand until softened. Remove the chilies from the water with a slotted spoon. Cut away and discard the stem and seeds, then cut into thin strips.

2 Place the seasoned flour in a large bowl. Add the beef and toss to coat well. Remove the beef from the bowl, shaking off the excess flour.

3 Heat the oil in a skillet. Add the beef and brown briefly over high heat. Reduce the heat to medium, add the onions and garlic, and cook for 2 minutes.

4 Add the tomatoes, reconstituted chilies or the bottled chipotle salsa, and stock, then cover and let simmer over low heat for 1½ hours, or until the meat is very tender, adding the green beans and sugar 15 minutes before the end of the cooking time. Skim off any fat that rises to the surface every now and again.

5 Transfer to individual bowls and serve with simmered beans and rice.

1½ dried chipotle chilies
or a few shakes of bottled
chipotle salsa
about 3 tbsp all-purpose flour,
well seasoned with salt and
pepper, for coating
2 lb 4 oz/1 kg stewing beef,
cut into large bite-size pieces
2 tbsp vegetable oil
2 onions, chopped
5 garlic cloves, chopped
14 oz/400 g tomatoes, diced
generous 6⅓ cups beef stock
12 oz/350 g green beans
pinch of sugar

TO SERVE
simmered beans
freshly cooked rice

Meatballs in Spicy-Sweet Sauce

prepare 20 minutes

cook 20 minutes

serves 4

1 cup fresh ground pork

1 cup fresh ground beef or lamb

6 tbsp cooked rice or finely
   crushed tortilla chips

1 egg, lightly beaten

1½ onions, very finely chopped

5 garlic cloves,
   very finely chopped

½ tsp ground cumin

large pinch of ground cinnamon

2 tbsp raisins

2 tbsp vegetable oil,
   plus extra if needed

2 sweet potatoes, peeled and cut
   into small chunks

salt and pepper

SPICY-SWEET SAUCE

1 tbsp molasses

1–2 tbsp cider or wine vinegar

14 oz/400 g canned tomatoes,
   drained and chopped

1½ cups beef stock

1–2 tbsp mild chili powder,
   such as ancho or New Mexico

1 tbsp paprika

1 tbsp chopped fresh cilantro

1 tbsp chopped fresh parsley
   or mint

TO SERVE

grated cheese

lightly cooked green beans
   (optional)

Called *albondigas* in Mexico, these tasty meatballs are set off brilliantly against the rich sauce and golden sweet potatoes.

1 Mix the meat thoroughly with the rice, the egg, half the onion and garlic, the cumin, cinnamon, and raisins.

2 Divide the mixture into even-size pieces and roll into balls. Pan-fry the balls in a nonstick skillet over medium heat, adding a little oil, if necessary, to help them brown. Remove the balls from the skillet and set aside. Wipe the skillet clean.

3 To make the sauce, place the molasses in a food processor or blender with the vinegar, tomatoes, stock, chili powder, paprika, and remaining onion and garlic. Process until blended, then stir in the cilantro and parsley. Set aside.

4 Heat the oil in the cleaned skillet. Add the sweet potatoes and cook until tender and golden brown, adding more oil if needed. Pour in the blended sauce and add the meatballs to the skillet. Cook for 10 minutes, or until the meatballs are heated through and the flavors have combined. Season to taste with salt and pepper. Sprinkle with grated cheese and serve with green beans, if wished.

Burritos of Lamb & Black Beans

 prepare 15 minutes,
plus 4 hours' marinating
cook 15–20 minutes
serves 4

1 lb 7 oz/650 g lean lamb
3 garlic cloves,
  very finely chopped
juice of ½ lime
½ tsp mild chili powder,
  such as ancho or New Mexico
½ tsp ground cumin
large pinch of dried oregano
  leaves, crushed
1–2 tbsp extra virgin olive oil
4 large flour tortillas
scant 2⅓ cups cooked black
  beans, seasoned with a little
  cumin, salt, and pepper
2–3 tbsp chopped fresh cilantro,
  plus a few sprigs to garnish
salt and pepper
salsa, preferably Chipotle Salsa
lime wedges, to serve (optional)

Stir-fried marinated lamb strips are paired with earthy black beans in these tasty burritos.

1 Slice the lamb into thin strips, then combine with the garlic, lime juice, chili powder, cumin, oregano, and oil in a nonmetallic bowl. Season to taste with salt and pepper. Cover and let marinate in the refrigerator for 4 hours.

2 To warm the tortillas, heat an unoiled nonstick skillet, add a tortilla, and heat through, sprinkling with a few drops of water as it heats. Wrap in foil or a clean dish towel to keep warm. Repeat with the other tortillas.

3 Warm the black beans with a little water in a pan.

4 Stir-fry the lamb in a heavy-bottom nonstick skillet over high heat until browned on all sides. Remove the skillet from the heat.

5 Spoon some of the beans and browned meat into a tortilla, sprinkle with cilantro, then add a little salsa and fold in the sides. Repeat with the remaining tortillas. Garnish with cilantro sprigs and serve immediately with lime wedges and any spare salsa, if wished.

Chili Verde

If tomatillos are not available, use fresh tomatoes and bottled green salsa instead, and add a good hit of lime juice at the end.

 prepare 15 minutes
cook 2 hours
serves 4

1 Place the pork in a large ovenproof casserole with the onion, bay leaves, and garlic bulb. Add water to cover and the bouillon cube and bring to a boil. Skim off the scum that rises to the surface, reduce the heat to very low, and let simmer gently for 1½ hours, or until the meat is very tender.

2 Meanwhile, place the chopped garlic in a food processor or blender with the tomatillos and chilies. Process to a purée.

3 Heat the oil in a deep sauté pan. Add the tomatillo mixture and cook over medium–high heat for 10 minutes, or until thickened. Add the stock, chili powder, and cumin.

4 When the meat is tender, remove from the casserole and add to the sauce. Let simmer gently for 20 minutes, or until the flavors are combined.

5 Garnish with the chopped cilantro and serve with warmed tortillas and lime wedges.

2 lb 4 oz/1 kg pork,
  cut into bite-size chunks
1 onion, chopped
2 bay leaves
1 whole garlic bulb, cut in half
1 bouillon cube
2 garlic cloves, chopped
1 lb/450 g fresh tomatillos,
  husks removed, cooked in a
  small amount of water until
  just tender, then chopped,
  or canned
2 large fresh mild green chilies,
  such as poblano, or a
  combination of 1 green bell
  pepper and 2 jalapeño chilies,
  seeded and chopped
3 tbsp vegetable oil, for cooking
1 cup pork or chicken stock
½ tsp mild chili powder,
such as ancho or New Mexico
½ tsp ground cumin
4–6 tbsp chopped fresh cilantro,
  to garnish

TO SERVE
4 flour tortillas
lime wedges

Spicy Pork & Vegetable Guisado

prepare 10 minutes

cook 2 hours

serves 4

This is a stew of southern climes, full of warm, sunny flavors. Mexican oregano is rather different to the Mediterranean variety, but the latter still works well here.

6 ripe tomatoes
1 lb/450 g lean boneless pork, cut into 1-inch/2.5-cm cubes
all-purpose flour, well seasoned with salt and pepper, for coating
1 tbsp vegetable oil, for cooking
8 oz/225 g chorizo sausage, outer casing removed, cut into bite-size chunks
1 onion, coarsely chopped
4 garlic cloves, very finely chopped
2 celery stalks, chopped
1 cinnamon stick, broken
2 bay leaves
2 tsp allspice
2 carrots, sliced
2–3 fresh red chilies, such as Thai, seeded and very finely chopped
4 cups pork or vegetable stock
2 sweet potatoes, cut into chunks
corn kernels, cut from 1 corncob
1 tbsp chopped fresh oregano
salt and pepper
fresh oregano sprigs, to garnish
freshly cooked rice, to serve

1 Place the tomatoes in a heatproof bowl and pour over boiling water to cover. Let stand for 1–2 minutes, then remove the tomatoes with a slotted spoon, peel off the skins, and refresh in cold water. Chop the flesh and place in a large, nonmetallic bowl.

2 Toss the pork in the seasoned flour to coat. Heat the oil in a large, heavy-bottom pan or ovenproof casserole. Add the chorizo and lightly brown on all sides. Remove the chorizo with a slotted spoon and set aside.

3 Add the pork, in batches, and cook until browned on all sides. Remove the pork with a slotted spoon and set aside. Add the onion, garlic, and celery to the pan and cook for 5 minutes, or until softened.

4 Add the cinnamon, bay leaves, and allspice and cook, stirring, for 2 minutes. Add the pork, carrots, chilies, tomatoes, and stock. Bring to a boil, then reduce the heat, cover, and let simmer for 1 hour, or until the pork is tender.

5 Return the chorizo to the pan with the sweet potatoes, corn, oregano, and salt and pepper to taste. Cover and let simmer for an additional 30 minutes, or until the vegetables are tender. Garnish with oregano leaves and serve with rice.

Carnitas

 prepare 15 minutes,
plus 30 minutes' cooling

cook 2½ hours

serves 4–6

2 lb 4 oz/1 kg pork, such as
   lean belly (side pork)
1 onion, chopped
1 whole garlic bulb, cut in half
½ tsp ground cumin
2 meat bouillon cubes
2 bay leaves
salt and pepper
fresh chili strips, to garnish

TO SERVE
freshly cooked rice
Refried Beans
salsa of your choice

In this classic Mexican dish, pieces of pork are first simmered to make them meltingly tender, then browned until irresistibly crisp.

1 Place the pork in a heavy-bottom pan with the onion, garlic, cumin, bouillon cubes, and bay leaves. Add water to cover. Bring to a boil, then reduce the heat to very low. Skim off the scum that rises to the surface.

2 Continue to cook very gently for 2 hours, or until the pork is tender. Remove from the heat and let the pork cool in the liquid.

3 Remove the pork from the pan with a slotted spoon. Cut off any rind. Cut the pork into bite-size pieces and sprinkle with salt and pepper to taste. Set aside 1¼ cups of the cooking liquid.

4 Brown the pork in a heavy-bottom skillet for 15 minutes, to cook off the fat. Add the reserved cooking liquid and allow to reduce down. Continue to cook the meat for 15 minutes, covering the skillet to avoid splattering. Turn the pork every now and again.

5 Transfer the pork to a serving dish, garnish with chili strips, and serve with rice, Refried Beans, and salsa.

Tequila-Marinated Crisp Chicken Wings

The tequila tenderizes these tasty chicken wings and gives them a delicious flavor. Serve as part of a barbecue, accompanied by corn tortillas, refried beans, salsa, and lots of chilled lager.

 prepare 10 minutes, plus 3 hours' marinating
cook 15–20 minutes
serves 4

1 Cut the chicken wings into 2 pieces at the joint.

2 Place the chicken wings in a nonmetallic dish and add the remaining ingredients. Toss well to coat, then cover and let marinate in the refrigerator for at least 3 hours or overnight.

3 Preheat the barbecue. Cook the chicken wings over the hot coals of the barbecue for 15–20 minutes, or until crisply browned and the juices run clear when a skewer is inserted into the thickest part of the meat, turning occasionally. Alternatively, cook in a ridged stovetop grill pan. Serve immediately, with barbecued or broiled tomato halves, if wished.

2 lb/900 g chicken wings
11 garlic cloves,
  very finely chopped
juice of 2 limes
juice of 1 orange
2 tbsp tequila
1 tbsp mild chili powder,
  such as ancho or New Mexico
2 tsp Chipotle Salsa
2 tbsp vegetable oil
1 tsp sugar
¼ tsp ground allspice
pinch of ground cinnamon
pinch of ground cumin
pinch of dried oregano
barbecued or broiled tomato
  halves, to serve (optional)

Chicken Fajitas

 prepare 15 minutes,
plus 2–3 hours' marinating

cook 12–15 minutes

serves 4

MARINADE

3 tbsp olive oil

3 tbsp maple syrup or honey

1 tbsp red wine vinegar

2 garlic cloves, crushed

2 tsp dried oregano

1–2 tsp dried red bell
pepper flakes

salt and pepper

4 skinless, boneless
chicken breasts

2 red bell peppers, seeded and
cut into 1-inch/2.5-cm strips

8 flour tortillas, warmed

The secret of fajita success lies in marinating the meat prior to quick cooking. It may take a little forward planning but very little extra effort for a far superior result.

1 To make the marinade, place the oil, maple syrup, vinegar, garlic, oregano, red bell pepper flakes, and salt and pepper to taste in a large, shallow dish or bowl and mix together.

2 Slice the chicken across the grain into slices 1 inch/2.5 cm thick. Toss in the marinade until well coated. Cover and let chill in the refrigerator for 2–3 hours, turning occasionally.

3 Heat a stovetop ridged grill pan until hot. Lift the chicken slices from the marinade with a slotted spoon, lay on the grill pan, and cook over medium-high heat for 3–4 minutes on each side, or until cooked through. Remove the chicken to a warmed serving plate and keep warm.

4 Add the bell peppers, skin-side down, to the grill pan and cook for 2 minutes on each side. Transfer to the serving plate.

5 Serve immediately, with the warmed tortillas to be used as wraps.

Chicken Mole Poblano

 prepare 20 minutes

cook 1 hour 20 minutes

serves 4

3 tomatoes

3 tbsp olive oil

4 chicken pieces, about
   6 oz/175 g each, halved

1 onion, chopped

2 garlic cloves,
   very finely chopped

1 hot dried red chili, such as
   chipotle, very finely chopped

1 tbsp sesame seeds, toasted,
   plus extra to garnish

1 tbsp chopped almonds

¼ tsp each ground cinnamon,
cumin, and cloves

2 tbsp raisins

1½ cups chicken stock

1 tbsp peanut butter

1 oz/25 g semisweet chocolate
   with a high cocoa content,
   grated, plus extra to garnish

salt and pepper

This recipe features a famed sauce, Mole Poblano, renowned for its surprising pairing of chocolate and chili. The result is sumptuous rather than strange, with a deep, rich, mellow quality.

1 Place the tomatoes in a heatproof bowl and pour over boiling water to cover. Let stand for 1–2 minutes, then remove the tomatoes with a slotted spoon, peel off the skins, and refresh in cold water. Chop the flesh and place in a nonmetallic bowl.

2 Heat 2 tablespoons of the oil in a large skillet. Add the chicken and cook until browned on all sides. Remove the chicken pieces with a slotted spoon and set aside.

3 Add the onion, garlic, and chili and cook for 5 minutes, or until softened. Add the sesame seeds, almonds, and spices and cook, stirring, for 2 minutes. Add the tomatoes, raisins, stock, peanut butter, and chocolate and stir well. Season to taste with salt and pepper and let simmer for an additional 5 minutes.

4 Transfer the mixture to a food processor or blender and process until smooth (you may need to do this in batches).

5 Return the mixture to the skillet, add the chicken, and bring to a boil. Reduce the heat, cover, and let simmer for 1 hour, or until the chicken is very tender, adding more liquid if necessary.

6 Serve garnished with sesame seeds and a little grated chocolate.

Chicken Tacos from Puebla

Seasoned chicken fills these soft tacos, along with creamy refried beans, avocado, smoky chipotle, and sour cream. A feast of tastes!

 prepare 10 minutes
cook 15 minutes
serves 4

1 To warm the tortillas, heat an unoiled nonstick skillet, add a tortilla, and heat through, sprinkling with a few drops of water as it heats. Wrap in foil or a clean dish towel to keep warm. Repeat with the other tortillas.

2 Cut the avocado in half lengthwise and twist the 2 halves in opposite directions to separate. Stab the pit with the point of a sharp knife and lift out. Carefully peel off the skin, slice the flesh, and toss in lime juice to prevent discoloration.

3 Heat the oil in a skillet. Add the chicken and heat through. Season to taste with salt and pepper.

4 Meanwhile, place the refried beans in a pan with 2 tbsp water and heat through gently. Combine the warmed beans with the cumin and oregano.

5 Spread one tortilla with the refried beans, then top with a spoonful of the chicken, a slice or two of avocado, a little salsa, chipotle to taste, a dollop of sour cream, and a sprinkling of onion, lettuce, and radishes. Season to taste with salt and pepper, then roll up as tightly as you can. Repeat with the remaining tortillas and serve immediately.

8 soft corn tortillas
1 avocado
lime or lemon juice, for tossing
2 tsp vegetable oil
8–12 oz/225–350 g leftover
   cooked chicken, diced
   or shredded
1 quantity (or 8 oz/225 g
   canned) Refried Beans
¼ tsp ground cumin
¼ tsp dried oregano
salsa of your choice
1 canned chipotle chili in
   adobo marinade, chopped,
   or bottled chipotle salsa
¾ cup sour cream
½ onion, chopped
handful of lettuce leaves,
   such as romaine or iceberg
5 radishes, diced
salt and pepper

Chicken Tortilla Flutes with Guacamole

 prepare 15 minutes
cook 15 minutes
serves 4

8 soft corn tortillas
12 oz/350 g cooked chicken,
   diced
1 tsp mild chili powder,
   such as ancho or New Mexico
1 onion, chopped
2 tbsp very finely chopped
   fresh cilantro
1–2 tbsp sour cream
vegetable oil, for cooking
salt

TO SERVE
1 quantity Guacamole
salsa of your choice

In Mexcio, these crisply fried, rolled tortillas are known as *flautas*, meaning "flutes," because of their delicate, long shape.

1 To warm the tortillas, heat an unoiled nonstick skillet, add a tortilla, and heat through, sprinkling with a few drops of water as it heats. Wrap in foil or a clean dish towel to keep warm. Repeat with the other tortillas.

2 Place the chicken in a large bowl with the chili powder, half the chopped onion and cilantro, and salt to taste. Add enough sour cream to bind the mixture together.

3 Arrange 2 corn tortillas on the counter so that they are overlapping, then spoon some of the filling down the center. Roll up very tightly and secure in place with a toothpick or two. Repeat with the remaining tortillas and filling.

4 Heat enough oil for cooking in a deep skillet until hot and cook the rolls until golden and crisp. Carefully remove the rolls from the oil and then drain on paper towels.

5 Serve with the Guacamole, salsa, and the remaining onion and cilantro.

Chicken with Yucatecan Vinegar Sauce

 prepare 15 minutes,
plus 30 minutes' standing

cook 35–45 minutes

serves 4–6

8 small boned chicken thighs
chicken stock
15–20 garlic cloves, unpeeled
1 tsp coarsely ground
  black pepper
½ tsp ground cloves
2 tsp crumbled dried oregano
  or ½ tsp crushed bay leaves
about ½ tsp salt
1 tbsp lime juice
1 tsp cumin seeds,
  lightly toasted
1 tbsp all-purpose flour,
  plus extra for dredging
½ cup vegetable oil
3–4 onions, thinly sliced
2 fresh chilies, preferably
  mild yellow ones, such as
  Mexican Guero or similar
  Turkish or Greek chilies,
  seeded and sliced
generous ⅓ cup cider or
  sherry vinegar

TO SERVE
mixed salad
lime wedges

A paste of roasted garlic and mixed spices gives an evocative flavor to this tangy dish of simmered chicken, a specialty of Valladolid in the Yucatán peninsula.

1 Place the chicken in a pan with enough stock to cover. Bring to a boil, then reduce the heat and let simmer for 5 minutes. Remove from the heat and allow the chicken to continue to cook while cooling in the stock.

2 Meanwhile, roast the garlic in an unoiled skillet until the cloves are browned and the inside tender. Remove from the heat. When cool enough to handle, squeeze the flesh from the skins and place in a bowl.

3 Using a mortar and pestle, grind the garlic with the pepper, cloves, oregano, salt, lime juice, and three-quarters of the cumin seeds. Mix with the flour. Remove the chicken from the stock, reserving the stock, and pat dry. Rub with two-thirds of the spice paste. Cover and let stand at room temperature for 30 minutes or overnight in the refrigerator.

4 Heat a little of the oil in a skillet and cook the onions and chilies until golden brown and softened. Pour in the vinegar and remaining cumin seeds, cook for a few minutes, then add the reserved stock and remaining spice paste. Boil, stirring, for 10 minutes, or until reduced in volume.

5 Dredge the chicken with flour. Heat the remaining oil in a skillet. Pan-fry the chicken until lightly browned and the juices run clear when a skewer is inserted into the thickest part. Serve topped with the sauce, with a mixed salad, and with lime wedges to squeeze over.

Chicken Tostadas with Green Salsa & Chipotles

Chicken makes a delicate yet satisfying topping for crisp tostadas. You do not need to prepare chicken especially for this recipe—any leftover chicken can be used, just skip steps 2 and 3.

 prepare 20 minutes
cook 15 minutes
serves 4–6

1 To make the tostadas, cook the tortillas in a small amount of oil in a nonstick skillet until crisp. Set aside.

2 Place the chicken in a pan with the stock and garlic. Bring to a boil, then reduce the heat and cook for 1–2 minutes, or until the chicken begins to turn opaque.

3 Remove the chicken from the heat and let stand in its hot liquid to cook through.

4 Heat the beans in a separate pan with enough water to form a smooth purée. Add the cumin and keep warm.

5 Meanwhile, cut the avocado in half lengthwise and twist the 2 halves in opposite directions to separate. Stab the pit with the point of a sharp knife and lift out. Carefully peel off the skin, dice or slice the flesh, and toss in lime juice to prevent discoloration.

6 Reheat the tostadas under a preheated medium broiler, if necessary. Spread the hot beans on the tostadas, then sprinkle with the cheese. Lift the cooked chicken from the liquid and divide between the tostadas. Top with the chopped cilantro, tomatoes, lettuce, radishes, scallions, avocado, sour cream, and a few strips of chipotle. Serve immediately.

6 soft corn tortillas
vegetable oil
1 lb/450 g skinless, boneless chicken breast or thighs, cut into strips or small pieces
1 cup chicken stock
2 garlic cloves, very finely chopped
2 quantites (or 14 oz/400 g canned) Refried Beans
large pinch of ground cumin
1 ripe avocado
lime or lemon juice, for tossing
2 cups grated cheese
1 tbsp chopped fresh cilantro
2 ripe tomatoes, diced
handful of crisp lettuce leaves, such as romaine or iceberg, shredded
4–6 radishes, diced
3 scallions, thinly sliced
sour cream, to taste
1–2 canned chipotle chilies in adobo marinade, drained and cut into thin strips

Turkey with Mole

prepare 15 minutes

cook 1 hour 10 minutes–
1 hour 40 minutes

serves 4

4 turkey portions,
  each cut into 4 pieces
about 2 cups chicken stock,
  plus extra for thinning
about 1 cup water
1 onion, chopped
1 whole garlic bulb, divided into
  cloves and peeled
1 celery stalk, chopped
1 bay leaf
1 bunch fresh cilantro,
  very finely chopped
scant 2½ cups Mole Poblano or
  use ready-made mole paste,
  thinned as instructed on
  the container
4–5 tbsp sesame seeds,
  to garnish

In gourmet specialty stores you can buy a jar of mole paste—useful for when you don't have a stash of leftover homemade mole sauce in your refrigerator or freezer.

1 Preheat the oven to 375°F/190°C. Arrange the turkey in a large ovenproof casserole. Pour the stock and water around the turkey, then add the onion, garlic, celery, bay leaf, and half the cilantro.

2 Cover and bake in the preheated oven for 1–1½ hours, or until the turkey is very tender. Add extra liquid if needed.

3 Warm the Mole Poblano in a pan with enough stock to make it the consistency of thin cream.

4 To toast the sesame seeds for the garnish, place the seeds in an unoiled skillet and roast, shaking the skillet, until lightly golden.

5 Arrange the turkey pieces on a serving plate and spoon the warmed mole sauce over the top. Sprinkle with the toasted sesame seeds and the remaining chopped cilantro and serve.

Seafood Guisado

prepare 20 minutes,
plus 10 minutes' cooling

cook 50 minutes

serves 4

1 each of yellow, red,
  and orange bell peppers,
  seeded and quartered
1 lb/450 g ripe tomatoes
2 large fresh mild green chilies,
  such as poblano
6 garlic cloves, peeled
2 tsp dried oregano or dried
  mixed herbs
2 tbsp olive oil, plus extra
  for drizzling
1 large onion,
  very finely chopped
2 cups fish, vegetable,
  or chicken stock
finely grated rind and juice
  of 1 lime
2 tbsp chopped fresh cilantro,
  plus extra to garnish
1 bay leaf
1 lb/450 g red snapper fillets,
  skinned and cut into chunks
8 oz/225 g raw shrimp, shelled
  and deveined
8 oz/225 g cleaned squid,
  cut into rings
salt and pepper

Roasting the bell peppers, tomatoes, chilies, and garlic enhances the flavor of this sumptuous seafood medley. You can use any other firm fish fillets or a mixture, if you prefer.

1 Preheat the oven to 400°F/200°C. Place the bell pepper quarters, skin-side up, in a roasting pan with the tomatoes, chilies, and garlic. Sprinkle with the dried oregano and drizzle with oil.

2 Roast in the preheated oven for 30 minutes, or until the bell peppers are well browned and softened.

3 Remove the roasted vegetables from the oven and leave until cool enough to handle. Peel off the skins from the bell peppers, tomatoes, and chilies and chop the flesh. Mince the garlic.

4 Heat the oil in a large pan. Add the onion and cook for 5 minutes, or until softened. Add the bell peppers, tomatoes, chilies, garlic, stock, lime rind and juice, chopped cilantro, bay leaf, and salt and pepper to taste. Bring to a boil, then stir in the fish and seafood. Reduce the heat, cover, and let simmer gently for 10 minutes, or until the fish and seafood are just cooked through. Garnish with chopped cilantro before serving.

Pan-Fried Scallops Mexicana

Scallops, with their sweet flesh, are delicious with the citrus flavors of Mexico. Often they are prepared just this simply, served with wedges of lime to squeeze over as desired, and a stack of warm corn tortillas.

 prepare 5 minutes

cook 10 minutes

serves 4–6

1 Heat half the butter and oil in a large, heavy-bottom skillet until the butter foams.

2 Add the scallops and cook quickly until just turning opaque; do not overcook. Remove from the skillet with a slotted spoon and keep warm.

3 Add the remaining butter and oil to the skillet, then toss in the scallions and garlic and cook over medium heat until the scallions are wilted. Return the scallops to the skillet.

4 Remove the skillet from the heat and add the chili and chopped cilantro. Squeeze in the lime juice. Season to taste with salt and pepper and stir to mix well.

5 Serve immediately with lime wedges for squeezing over the scallops.

2 tbsp butter
2 tbsp virgin olive oil
1 lb 7 oz/650 g scallops, shelled
4–5 scallions, thinly sliced
3–4 garlic cloves,
  very finely chopped
½ fresh green chili, such as
  Anaheim or poblano, seeded
  and very finely chopped
2 tbsp very finely chopped
  fresh cilantro
juice of ½ lime
salt and pepper
lime wedges, to serve

Shrimp in Green Bean Sauce

prepare 10 minutes

cook 15–20 minutes

serves 4

2 tbsp vegetable oil

3 onions, chopped

5 garlic cloves, chopped

5–7 ripe tomatoes, diced

6–8 oz/175–225 g green beans,
  cut into 2-inch/5-cm pieces
  and blanched for 1 minute

¼ tsp ground cumin

pinch of ground allspice

pinch of ground cinnamon

½–1 canned chipotle chili
  in adobo marinade,
  with some of the marinade

2 cups fish stock or
  water mixed with
  1 fish bouillon cube

1 lb/450 g raw shrimp, shelled
  and deveined

chopped fresh cilantro,
  to garnish

1 lime, cut into wedges,
  to serve (optional)

The sweet, briny flesh of shrimp is wonderful paired with the smoky scent of chipotle chili.

1 Heat the oil in a large, deep skillet. Add the onions and garlic and cook over low heat for 5–10 minutes, or until softened. Add the tomatoes and cook for an additional 2 minutes.

2 Add the green beans, cumin, allspice, cinnamon, the chili and marinade, and stock. Bring to a boil, then reduce the heat and simmer for a few minutes to combine the flavors.

3 Add the shrimp and cook for 1–2 minutes only, then remove the skillet from the heat and let the shrimp steep in the hot liquid to finish cooking. They are cooked when they have turned a bright pink color.

4 Serve immediately, garnished with the chopped fresh cilantro and accompanied by the lime wedges, if using.

Chili-Shrimp Tacos

 prepare 20 minutes

cook 35 minutes

serves 4

1 lb 5 oz/600 g raw shrimp,
   shelled and deveined
2 tbsp chopped fresh
   flat-leaf parsley
12 taco shells
1 scallion, chopped, to garnish

TACO SAUCE
1 lb/450 g ripe tomatoes
1 tbsp olive oil
1 onion, very finely chopped
1 green bell pepper,
   seeded and diced
1–2 fresh hot green chilies,
   such as jalapeño, seeded
   and very finely chopped
3 garlic cloves, crushed
1 tsp ground cumin
1 tsp ground coriander
1 tsp brown sugar
juice of ½ lemon
salt and pepper

TO SERVE
sour cream
salsa of your choice

This is a gourmet, not to say healthy, take on a trusty favorite—ideal for an informal dinner party. Use cooked shrimp and just heat through gently in the sauce for an everyday option.

1 Place the tomatoes in a heatproof bowl and pour over enough boiling water to cover. Let stand for 1–2 minutes, then remove the tomatoes with a slotted spoon, peel off the skins, and refresh in cold water. Dice the flesh.

2 To make the sauce, heat the oil in a deep skillet over medium heat. Add the onion and cook for 5 minutes, or until softened. Add the bell pepper and chilies and cook for 5 minutes. Add the garlic, cumin, coriander, and sugar and cook the sauce for an additional 2 minutes, stirring. Add the tomatoes, lemon juice, and salt and pepper to taste. Bring to a boil, then reduce the heat and let simmer for 10 minutes.

3 Preheat the oven to 350°F/180°C. Stir the shrimp and parsley into the sauce, cover, and cook gently for 5–8 minutes, or until the shrimp are pink and tender.

4 Meanwhile, place the taco shells, open-side down, on a baking sheet. Warm in the preheated oven for 2–3 minutes.

5 Spoon the shrimp mixture into the taco shells, top with a spoonful of sour cream, and garnish with the chopped scallion. Serve with some salsa.

Fish Tacos Ensenada Style

These tacos of pan-fried fish chunks and red cabbage salad are served up in the *cantinas* and *fondas* of the coastal town of Ensenada, in Mexico's Baja California.

 prepare 15 minutes
cook 25 minutes
serves 4

1 Place the fish on a plate and sprinkle with half the oregano, cumin, chili powder, and garlic, and salt and pepper to taste. Dust with the flour.

2 In a nonmetallic bowl, combine the cabbage with the remaining oregano, cumin, chili powder, and garlic, then stir in the lime juice, and salt, and hot pepper sauce to taste. Set aside.

3 Heat the oil in a skillet until it is smoking, then pan-fry the fish in several batches until it is golden on the outside and just tender in the middle. Remove from the skillet and place on paper towels to drain.

4 To warm the tortillas, heat an unoiled nonstick skillet, add a tortilla, and heat through, sprinkling with a few drops of water as it heats. Wrap in foil or a clean dish towel to keep warm. Repeat with the other tortillas.

5 Place some of the warm pan-fried fish in each tortilla with a large spoonful of the hot cabbage salad. Sprinkle with chopped cilantro, and onion if using. Add some salsa and serve immediately.

about 1 lb/450 g firm-fleshed white fish, such as red snapper or cod
¼ tsp dried oregano
¼ tsp ground cumin
1 tsp mild chili powder, such as ancho or New Mexico
2 garlic cloves, very finely chopped
3 tbsp all-purpose flour
¼ head red cabbage, thinly sliced or shredded
juice of 2 limes
hot pepper sauce or salsa, to taste
vegetable oil
8 corn tortillas
1 tbsp chopped fresh cilantro
½ onion, chopped (optional)
salt and pepper
salsa of your choice, to serve

Swordfish with Yucatecan Flavors

 prepare 30 minutes,
plus 3 hours' marinating

cook 15 minutes

serves 8

4 tbsp annatto seeds,
    soaked in water overnight
3 garlic cloves,
    very finely chopped
1 tbsp mild chili powder,
    such as ancho or New Mexico
1 tbsp paprika
1 tsp ground cumin
½ tsp dried oregano
2 tbsp beer or tequila
juice of 1 lime and 1 orange
    or 3 tbsp pineapple juice
2 tbsp olive oil
2 tbsp chopped fresh cilantro
¼ tsp ground cinnamon
¼ tsp ground cloves
2 lb 4 oz/1 kg swordfish steaks
banana leaves, for wrapping
    (optional)
fresh cilantro sprigs, to garnish
orange wedges, to serve

Annatto seeds are rock-hard little red seeds that need to be soaked overnight before you can grind them. They have a distinctive lemony flavor and impart a dark orange color to the dish.

1 Drain the annatto seeds, then crush them to a paste with a mortar and pestle. Work in the garlic, chili powder, paprika, cumin, oregano, beer, fruit juice, oil, chopped cilantro, cinnamon, and cloves.

2 Smear the paste onto the fish, cover, and let marinate in the refrigerator for at least 3 hours or overnight.

3 Wrap the fish steaks in banana leaves, tying with string to make packages. Bring enough water to a boil in a steamer, then add a batch of packages to the top part of the steamer and steam for 15 minutes, or until the fish is cooked through. Keep warm while you cook the other batches.

4 Alternatively, cook the fish without wrapping in the banana leaves. To cook on the grill, place in a hinged basket, or on a rack, and cook over hot coals for 5–6 minutes on each side, or until cooked through. Or cook the fish under a preheated hot broiler for 5–6 minutes on each side, or until cooked through.

5 Garnish with cilantro sprigs and serve with orange wedges for squeezing over the fish.

Fish Fillets with Papaya Sauce

prepare 15 minutes

cook 20–25 minutes

serves 4

4 white fish fillets, such as
   sea bass, sole, or cod, about
   6 oz/175 g each, skinned
olive oil, for drizzling
juice of 1 lime
2 tbsp chopped fresh cilantro
salt and pepper
lime wedges, to garnish

PAPAYA SAUCE
1 large ripe papaya
1 tbsp freshly squeezed
   orange juice
1 tbsp freshly squeezed
   lime juice
1 tbsp olive oil
1–2 tsp Tabasco sauce

This is just about as light as it gets in Mexican cooking—white fish fillets simply seasoned and baked, accompanied by a tropical fruit sauce enlivened with a dash of hot pepper sauce.

1 Preheat the oven to 350°F/180°C. Place the fish in a shallow ovenproof dish. Drizzle with oil and squeeze over the lime juice. Sprinkle the chopped cilantro over the fish and season to taste with salt and pepper.

2 Cover the dish tightly with foil and bake in the preheated oven for 15–20 minutes, or until the fish is just flaking.

3 Meanwhile, to make the sauce, halve the papaya and scoop out the seeds. Peel the halves and chop the flesh. Place the flesh in a food processor or blender and add the orange and lime juices, oil, and Tabasco to taste. Process until smooth.

4 Transfer the sauce to a pan and heat through gently for 3–4 minutes. Season to taste with salt and pepper.

5 Serve the fish fillets, in their cooking juices, with the sauce spooned over, garnished with lime wedges.

Fish Burritos

You can use any seafood you like in this tasty Mexican snack. Tacos are eaten in the hand, like sandwiches.

 prepare 15 minutes,
plus 30 minutes' cooling
cook 10 minutes
serves 4–6

1 Season the fish to taste with salt and pepper, then place in a pan with the cumin, oregano, garlic, and enough stock to cover.

2 Bring to a boil, then cook for 1 minute. Remove the pan from the heat. Let the fish cool in the cooking liquid for 30 minutes.

3 Remove the fish from the liquid with a slotted spoon and break up into bite-size pieces. Place in a nonmetallic bowl, sprinkle with the lemon juice, and set aside.

4 Heat the tortillas in an unoiled nonstick skillet, sprinkling them with a few drops of water as they heat. Wrap the tortillas in foil or a clean dish towel as you work to keep them warm.

5 Arrange shredded lettuce in the middle of one tortilla, spoon on a few big chunks of the fish, then sprinkle with the tomatoes. Add some of the Salsa Cruda. Repeat with the other tortillas and serve immediately garnished with lemon slices.

about 1 lb/450 g firm-fleshed
  white fish, such as red
  snapper or cod
¼ tsp ground cumin
pinch of dried oregano
4 garlic cloves,
  very finely chopped
½ cup fish stock or water mixed
with 1 fish bouillon cube
juice of ½ lemon or lime
8 flour tortillas
2–3 romaine lettuce leaves,
  shredded
2 ripe tomatoes, diced
1 quantity Salsa Cruda
salt and pepper
lemon slices, to garnish

Spicy Broiled Salmon

 prepare 15 minutes,
plus 1 hour's marinating

cook 8 minutes

serves 4

The woody smoked flavors of the chipotle chili marinade are delicious brushed onto salmon for broiling.

4 salmon steaks, about
  6–8 oz/175–225 g each
lime slices, to garnish

MARINADE
4 garlic cloves,
  very finely chopped
2 tbsp extra virgin olive oil
pinch of ground allspice
pinch of ground cinnamon
juice of 2 limes
1–2 tsp marinade from canned
  chipotle chilies or bottled
  chipotle chili salsa
¼ tsp ground cumin
pinch of sugar
salt and pepper, to taste

TO SERVE
tomato wedges
3 scallions, very finely chopped
shredded lettuce, such as
  romaine or iceberg

1 To make the marinade, place all the ingredients in a nonmetallic bowl and stir.

2 Coat the salmon with the marinade, then transfer to a large, nonmetallic dish. Cover with plastic wrap and let marinate in the refrigerator for 1 hour.

3 Preheat the broiler to medium. Trasfer the salmon from the marinade to a broiler pan and cook under the hot broiler for 3–4 minutes on each side, or until cooked through. Alternatively, cook the salmon over hot coals on a grill until cooked through.

4 To serve, mix the tomato wedges with the scallions. Place the salmon on 4 plates and arrange the tomato salad and shredded lettuce alongside. Garnish with lime slices and serve immediately.

Spinach & Mushroom Chimichangas

 **prepare** 20 minutes

cook 35 minutes

serves 4

2 tbsp olive oil, for cooking
1 large onion,
   very finely chopped
8 oz/225 g small mushrooms,
   finely sliced
2 fresh mild green chilies,
   seeded and very finely
   chopped
2 garlic cloves,
   very finely chopped
5⅝ cups spinach leaves,
   torn into pieces if large
6 oz/175 g Cheddar cheese,
   grated
8 flour tortillas
vegetable oil, for deep-frying

These crisp, deep-fried packages are universally appealing and are speedy to make. For an alternative meat filling, try the Chili con Carne topped with chopped onion and grated cheese.

1 Heat the oil in a large, heavy-bottom skillet. Add the onion and cook over medium heat for 5 minutes, or until softened.

2 Add the mushrooms, chilies, and garlic and cook for 5 minutes, or until the mushrooms are lightly browned. Add the spinach and cook, stirring, for 1–2 minutes, or until just wilted. Add the cheese and stir until just melted.

3 Meanwhile, to warm the tortillas, heat an unoiled nonstick skillet, add a tortilla, and heat through, sprinkling with a few drops of water as it heats. Wrap in foil or a clean dish towel to keep warm. Repeat with the other tortillas.

4 Spoon an equal quantity of the mixture into the center of each tortilla. Fold in 2 opposite sides of each tortilla to cover the filling, then roll up to enclose it completely.

5 Heat the oil for deep-frying in a deep-fryer or large, deep pan to 350–375°F/180–190°C, or until a cube of bread browns in 30 seconds. Deep-fry the chimichangas 2 at a time, turning once, for 5–6 minutes, or until crisp and golden. Drain on paper towels before serving.

Vegetable Tostadas

Top a crisp tostada with spicy vegetables and you have a fabulous vegetarian feast!

 prepare 10 minutes

cook 20 minutes

serves 4

1 To make the tostadas, pan-fry the tortillas in a small amount of oil in a nonstick skillet until crisp. Set aside.

2 Heat the remaining oil in the skillet. Add the potatoes and carrot and cook for 10 minutes, or until softened. Add the garlic, red bell pepper, chili powder, paprika, and cumin. Cook for 2–3 minutes, or until the bell peppers have softened.

3 Add the tomatoes, green beans, and oregano. Cook for 8–10 minutes, or until the vegetables are tender and form a saucelike mixture. The mixture should not be too dry; add a little water if necessary to keep it moist.

4 Preheat the broiler to medium. Heat the black beans in a pan with a tiny amount of water and keep warm. Reheat the tostadas under the hot broiler.

5 Spread the beans over the hot tostadas, then sprinkle with the cheese and top with a few spoonfuls of the hot vegetables in sauce. Sprinkle each tostada with the lettuce and scallions and serve immediately.

4 soft corn tortillas

3–4 tbsp virgin olive oil or vegetable oil

2 potatoes, diced

1 carrot, diced

3 garlic cloves, very finely chopped

1 red bell pepper, seeded and diced

1 tsp mild chili powder, such as ancho or New Mexico

1 tsp paprika

½ tsp ground cumin

3–4 ripe tomatoes, diced

4 oz/115 g green beans, blanched and cut into bite-size lengths

several large pinches of dried oregano

2⅓ cups cooked black beans, drained

8 oz/225 g feta cheese (drained weight), crumbled

3–4 romaine lettuce leaves, shredded

3–4 scallions, thinly sliced

Cheese Enchiladas with Mole Flavors

 prepare 15 minutes

cook 25–30 minutes

serves 4–6

8 soft corn tortillas

2 cups Mole Poblano or bottled
  mole paste

about 8 oz/225 g cheese,
  such as Cheddar, mozzarella,
  Asiago, or Mexican queso
  Oaxaca—one type or a
  combination, grated

1 cup chicken or vegetable stock

1 avocado

5 scallions, thinly sliced

2–3 tbsp chopped fresh cilantro

handful of romaine lettuce
  leaves, shredded

4 tbsp sour cream

salsa of your choice

Mole sauce makes a delicious enchilada—a good reason to make yourself a big pot of Mole Poblano. But if you are short of time, you can always use bottled mole paste instead.

1 Preheat the oven to 375°F/190°C. To warm the tortillas, heat an unoiled nonstick skillet, add a tortilla, and heat through, sprinkling with a few drops of water as it heats. Wrap in foil or a clean dish towel to keep warm. Repeat with the other tortillas.

2 Dip the tortillas into the Mole Poblano and pile up on a plate. Fill the inside of the top sauced tortilla with a few spoonfuls of grated cheese. Roll up and arrange in a shallow ovenproof dish. Repeat with the remaining tortillas, reserving a handful of the cheese to sprinkle over the top.

3 Pour the rest of the Mole Poblano over the rolled tortillas, then pour the stock over the top. Sprinkle with the reserved cheese and cover with foil.

4 Bake in the preheated oven for 20 minutes, or until the tortillas are piping hot and the cheese melted.

5 Meanwhile, cut the avocado in half lengthwise and twist the 2 halves in opposite directions to separate. Stab the pit with the point of a sharp knife and lift out. Carefully peel off the skin and dice the flesh.

6 Arrange the scallions, chopped cilantro, lettuce, avocado, and sour cream on top. Add salsa to taste. Serve immediately.

SIDE DISHES & SAUCES

Chilied Cornbread

prepare 10 minutes
cook 40–45 minutes
serves 8

scant 1 cup cornmeal
½ cup all-purpose flour
3 tsp baking powder
1 small onion,
  very finely chopped
1–2 fresh green chilies,
  such as serrano,
  seeded and chopped
4 tbsp corn or vegetable oil
4½ oz/125 g canned creamed-
  style corn kernels
1 cup sour cream
2 eggs, beaten

This is authentic chuck-wagon fare that will satisfy any hearty appetite. If you fancy a cheesy version, add ¾ cup grated Cheddar cheese to the mixture and sprinkle extra on top before baking.

1 Preheat the oven to 350°F/180°C.

2 Place the cornmeal, flour, and baking powder in a large bowl, then stir in the onion and chilies.

3 Heat the oil in a 9-inch/23-cm heavy-bottom skillet with a heatproof handle, tipping the skillet to coat the bottom and sides with the oil.

4 Make a well in the center of the ingredients in the bowl. Add the corn, sour cream, and eggs, then pour in the hot oil from the skillet. Stir lightly until combined. Pour into the hot skillet and smooth the surface.

5 Bake in the preheated oven for 35–40 minutes, or until a wooden toothpick inserted into the center comes out clean. Cut into wedges and serve warm from the skillet.

Quick Tomato Sauce

prepare 5–10 minutes

cook 15 minutes

serves 4–6

2 tbsp vegetable or olive oil
1 onion, thinly sliced
5 garlic cloves, thinly sliced
14 oz/400 g canned tomatoes,
   diced, plus their juices,
   or 1 lb 5 oz/600 g fresh
   diced tomatoes
several shakes of mild chili
   powder, such as ancho or
   New Mexico
1½ cups vegetable or chicken
   stock
salt and pepper
pinch of sugar (optional)

Simple to make, this versatile sauce is not only a great accompaniment for grilled meat and fish but also invaluable for baked tortilla dishes and taco fillings.

1 Heat the oil in a large skillet. Add the onion and garlic and cook for 3 minutes, or until just softened, stirring constantly.

2 Add the tomatoes, chili powder to taste, and the stock. Cook over medium–high heat for 10 minutes, or until the tomatoes have reduced slightly and the flavor of the sauce is more concentrated.

3 Season the sauce to taste with salt, pepper, and sugar, if using. Serve the dish warm.

Corn & Red Bell Pepper Salsa

This salsa has lots of natural texture and a sweet-and-sour taste. Use a large fresh green chili in place of the bottled chilies, if you prefer, or use half a red onion instead of the scallions.

 prepare 10 minutes, plus 30 minutes' chilling
cook no cooking required
serves 4–6

1 Drain the corn and place in a large, nonmetallic bowl.

2 Add the red bell pepper, garlic, chilies, scallions, lemon juice, oil, and chopped cilantro, then season to taste with salt and stir well to combine.

3 Cover and let chill in the refrigerator for at least 30 minutes to allow the flavors to develop before serving.

1 lb/450 g canned corn kernels
1 large red bell pepper, seeded and diced
1 garlic clove, crushed
1–2 tbsp very finely chopped bottled jalapeño chilies, or to taste
4 scallions, very finely chopped
2 tbsp lemon juice
1 tbsp olive oil
1 tbsp chopped fresh cilantro
salt

Hot Tomato Sauce

🌀 prepare 5–10 minutes
cook no cooking required
serves 4

This tangy sauce is excellent with crispy tortillas and tostadas, or with broiled or pan-fried fish.

2–3 fresh green chilies,
   such as jalapeño or serrano
8 oz/225 g canned chopped
   tomatoes
1 scallion, thinly sliced
2 garlic cloves, chopped
2–3 tbsp cider vinegar
¼–⅓ cup water
large pinch of dried oregano
large pinch of ground cumin
large pinch of sugar
large pinch of salt

1 Slice the chilies open, remove the seeds if wished, then chop the chilies.

2 Place the chilies in a food processor or blender with the tomatoes, scallion, garlic, cider vinegar, water, oregano, cumin, sugar, and salt. Process until smooth.

3 Adjust the seasoning, cover, and let chill until ready to serve. The sauce will keep for up to 1 week, covered, in the refrigerator.

Mole Verde

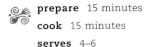

prepare 15 minutes

cook 15 minutes

serves 4–6

1⅛ cups toasted pumpkin seeds
  (pepitas)
4 cups chicken stock
several pinches of ground cloves
8–10 tomatillos, diced, or use
  1 cup mild tomatillo salsa
½ onion, chopped
½ fresh green chili, such as
  jalapeño or serrano, seeded
  and diced
3 garlic cloves, chopped
½ tsp fresh thyme leaves
½ tsp fresh marjoram leaves
3 tbsp shortening or vegetable
  oil, for cooking
3 bay leaves
4 tbsp chopped fresh cilantro
salt and pepper
fresh green chili slices,
  to garnish

Moles are purées and, depending on the ingredients, vary in color from yellow and green to chocolate brown. This green mole is a specialty of Jalisco. Serve with warm tortillas or unfilled tamales.

1 Grind the toasted pumpkin seeds (pepitas) in a food processor. Add half the stock, the cloves, tomatillos, onion, chili, garlic, thyme, and marjoram and blend to a purée.

2 Heat the shortening in a heavy-bottom skillet and add the puréed pumpkin seed mixture and the bay leaves. Cook over medium–high heat for 5 minutes, or until the mixture begins to thicken.

3 Remove the skillet from the heat and add the remaining stock and the chopped cilantro. Return the skillet to the heat and cook until the sauce thickens, then remove from the heat.

4 Remove the bay leaves and place the sauce in the food processor and process until completely smooth. Add salt and pepper to taste.

5 Transfer to a serving bowl, garnish with chili slices, and serve.

Pico de Gallo Salsa

This is the most famous Mexican salsa, its name translating as "rooster's beak"—apparently because it was traditionally eaten between the thumb and index finger, pecking-style.

 prepare 10 minutes, plus 30 minutes' chilling
cook no cooking required
serves 4–6

1 Place the diced tomatoes a large, nonmetallic bowl.

2 Add the onion, chili, chopped cilantro, and lime juice. Season to taste with salt and pepper and stir gently to combine.

3 Cover and let chill in the refrigerator for at least 30 minutes to allow the flavors to develop before serving.

3 large, ripe tomatoes,
  seeded and diced
½ red onion,
  very finely chopped
1 large fresh green chili,
  such as jalapeño, seeded
  and very finely chopped
2 tbsp chopped fresh cilantro
juice of 1 lime, or to taste
salt and pepper

Cooked Chipotle Salsa

prepare 15 minutes

cook 10 minutes

serves 4

3 dried chipotle chilies

1 onion, very finely chopped

14 oz/400 g canned tomatoes,
   including their juices

2–3 tbsp brown sugar

2–3 garlic cloves,
   very finely chopped

pinch of ground cinnamon

pinch of ground cloves
   or allspice

large pinch of ground cumin

juice of ½ lemon

1 tbsp extra virgin olive oil

salt

finely pared strips of lemon
   rind, to garnish

4 soft tortillas, to serve

This rich, tomato-red chipotle salsa is sweet and piquant, delicious with anything grilled, or dabbed into a taco or burrito.

1 Place the chilies in a pan with enough water to cover. Protecting your face against fumes and making sure that the kitchen is well ventilated, bring the chilies and water to a boil. Cook for 5 minutes, then remove the pan from the heat, cover, and let stand until softened.

2 Remove the chilies from the water with a slotted spoon. Cut away and discard the stem and seeds, then either scrape the flesh from the skins or chop up the whole chilies.

3 Place the onion in a pan with the tomatoes and sugar and cook over medium heat, stirring, until thickened.

4 Remove the pan from the heat and add the garlic, cinnamon, cloves, cumin, lemon juice, oil, and prepared chipotle chilies. Season to taste with salt and let cool. Serve with tortillas and garnished with lemon rind.

Pineapple & Mango Salsa

 prepare 15 minutes,
plus 30 minutes' chilling

cook no cooking required

serves 4

½ ripe pineapple

1 ripe mango

2 tbsp chopped fresh mint

2 tsp brown sugar

juice of 1 lime

1–2 tsp Tabasco sauce or
  Habañero sauce, or to taste

1 large tomato,
  seeded and diced

salt

mint sprigs, to garnish

Full of tropical fruit flavors, this exotic salsa provides a lively flavor contrast to robust savory Mexican fare. You could substitute a papaya for the mango for a slightly different taste experience.

1 Slice the pineapple, then peel the slices and remove the cores. Dice the flesh and place in a nonmetallic bowl with any juice.

2 Slice the mango lengthwise on either side of the flat central seed. Peel the 2 mango pieces and dice the flesh. Slice and peel any remaining flesh around the seed, then dice. Add to the pineapple with any juice.

3 Add the chopped mint, sugar, lime juice, Tabasco, and tomato, then season to taste with salt and stir well to combine. Cover and let chill in the refrigerator for at least 30 minutes to allow the flavors to develop. Stir again before serving, then garnish with mint sprigs.

Two Classic Salsas

A Mexican meal is not complete without a salsa. These two traditional salsas are ideal for seasoning any dish, from filled tortillas to broiled meat—they add a spicy hotness that is the very essence of Mexican cooking.

 prepare 5 minutes
cook no cooking required
serves 4–6

1 To make the Jalapeño Salsa, place the onion in a nonmetallic bowl with the garlic, chilies, lemon juice, and cumin. Season to taste with salt and stir together. Cover and let chill until required.

2 To make a chunky-textured Salsa Cruda, stir all the ingredients together in a nonmetallic bowl. Cover and let chill until required.

3 To make a smoother-textured salsa, process the ingredients in a food processor or blender. Cover and let chill until required.

JALAPEÑO SALSA
1 onion, very finely chopped
2–3 garlic cloves,
  very finely chopped
4–6 tbsp coarsely chopped
  pickled jalapeño chilies
juice of ½ lemon
about ¼ tsp ground cumin
salt, to taste

SALSA CRUDA
6–8 ripe tomatoes,
  very finely chopped
generous ⅓ cup tomato juice
3–4 garlic cloves,
  very finely chopped
½–1 bunch fresh cilantro leaves,
  coarsely chopped
pinch of sugar
3–4 fresh green chilies, such
  as jalapeño or serrano, seeded
  and very finely chopped
½–1 tsp ground cumin
3–4 scallions,
  very finely chopped
salt, to taste

Hot Mexican Salsas

These salsas capture the inimitable tangy, spicy flavor of Mexico. Choose from a fresh minty fruit salsa, charred chili salsa, or a spicy "green" salsa.

TROPICAL FRUIT SALSA

½ sweet ripe pineapple

1 mango or papaya

½–1 fresh green chili,
  such as jalapeño or serrano

½–1 fresh red chili

½ red onion, chopped

1 tbsp sugar

juice of 1 lime

3 tbsp chopped fresh mint

salt, to taste

SCORCHED CHILI SALSA

1 green bell pepper

2–3 fresh green chilies,
  such as jalapeño or serrano

2 garlic cloves, chopped

juice of ½ lime

1 tsp salt

2–3 tbsp olive oil

large pinch of dried oregano

large pinch of ground cumin

SALSA VERDE

1 lb/450 g canned tomatillos

1–2 fresh green chilies,
  such as jalapeño or serrano

1 green bell pepper

1 small onion, chopped

1 bunch fresh cilantro leaves,
  very finely chopped

½ tsp ground cumin

salt, to taste

1 To make the Tropical Fruit Salsa, peel the pineapple, cut out the core, then dice the flesh. Put into a large nonmetallic bowl with any juice.

2 Slice the mango lengthwise on either side of the flat central seed. Peel the 2 mango pieces and dice the flesh. Slice and peel any remaining flesh around the seed, then dice. Alternatively, halve the papaya and scoop out the seeds. Peel the halves and chop the flesh. Add to the pineapple with any juice.

3 Seed and chop the green chili and chop the red chili, then add with the remaining ingredients to the fruit. Cover the bowl and let chill until required.

4 For the Scorched Chili Salsa, roast the bell pepper and chilies in an unoiled skillet until the skins are charred. Place in a plastic bag, twist to seal well, then let stand for 20 minutes. Peel, seed, and chop the vegetables. Mix with the garlic, lime juice, salt, and oil in a nonmetallic bowl. Top with oregano and cumin.

5 For the Salsa Verde, drain and chop the tomatillos, seed and chop the green chilies and green bell pepper, and combine with the rest of the ingredients in a nonmetallic bowl. If a smoother sauce is preferred, process the ingredients in a food processor until blended. Spoon into a bowl to serve.

Chipotle Salsa

 prepare 5 minutes

cook no cooking required

serves 4–6

1 lb/450 g ripe juicy tomatoes,
  diced
3–5 garlic cloves,
  very finely chopped
½ bunch fresh cilantro leaves,
  coarsely chopped
1 small onion, chopped
1–2 tsp adobo marinade from
  canned chipotle chilies
½–1 tsp sugar
lime juice
pinch each of ground cinnamon,
  ground allspice, and ground
  cumin (all optional)
salt

Chipotles are the smoked jalapeño chili sold either dried or in cans, packed in a spicy flavorful marinade called adobo. Here the marinade from the canned version is used to perk up a simple fresh tomato salsa.

1 Place the tomatoes, garlic, and chopped cilantro in a food processor or blender.

2 Process the mixture until smooth, then add the onion, adobo marinade, and sugar.

3 Squeeze in lime juice to taste. Season to taste with salt, then add the cinnamon, allspice, and cumin, if using.

4 Serve immediately, or cover and let chill until ready to serve, although the salsa is at its best when served freshly made.

Mild Red Chili Sauce

This milder sauce is ideal for enchiladas and stewed meat. Keep some stashed in your freezer at all times for an instant hit of Mexico!

 prepare 10 minutes,
plus 20 minutes' cooling
cook 15–20 minutes
makes about 1½ cups

1 Using metal tongs, roast each chili over an open flame for a few seconds until the color darkens on all sides. Alternatively, place the chilies under a preheated hot broiler, turning them frequently.

2 Place the chilies in a heatproof bowl and pour boiling water over them. Cover and let the chilies cool for 20 minutes.

3 Meanwhile, place the stock in a pan and bring to a simmer.

4 When the chilies have cooled and are swelled up and softened, remove from the water with a slotted spoon. Remove the seeds from the chilies, then cut or tear the flesh into pieces and place in a food processor or blender. Process to a purée, then mix in the hot stock.

5 Place the chili and stock mixture in a pan. Purée the masa harina with enough water to make a thin paste, then add along with the cumin, garlic, and lime juice. Bring to a boil and cook for a few minutes, stirring, until the sauce has thickened. Add salt to taste, if necessary, and serve.

5 large fresh mild chilies,
  such as New Mexico or ancho
2 cups vegetable or
  chicken stock
1 tbsp masa harina or
  1 crumbled corn tortilla
large pinch of ground cumin
1–2 garlic cloves,
  very finely chopped
juice of 1 lime
salt

Guacamole

prepare 15 minutes

cook no cooking required

serves 4

2 large, ripe avocados

juice of 1 lime, or to taste

2 tsp olive oil

½ onion, very finely chopped

1 fresh mild green chili,
 such as poblano, seeded
 and very finely chopped

1 garlic clove, crushed

¼ tsp ground cumin

1 tbsp chopped fresh cilantro,
 plus extra to garnish (optional)

salt and pepper

There are as many versions of this dish as there are cooks, but a good result always depends on using quality, ripe avocados. Mashing rather than puréeing gives control over the texture.

1 Cut the avocados in half lengthwise and twist the 2 halves in opposite directions to separate. Stab the pit with the point of a sharp knife and lift out.

2 Peel, then coarsely chop the avocado halves and place in a nonmetallic bowl. Squeeze over the lime juice and add the oil.

3 Mash the avocados with a fork until the desired consistency—either chunky or smooth—is obtained. Stir in the onion, chili, garlic, cumin, and chopped cilantro, then season to taste with salt and pepper.

4 Transfer to a serving dish and serve immediately, to avoid discoloration, sprinkled with extra chopped cilantro, if liked.

Mole Poblano

prepare 20 minutes,
plus 1 hour's standing
cook 15 minutes
serves 8–10

3 dried mulato chilies
3 dried mild ancho chilies
5–6 dried New Mexico or
 California chilies
1 onion, chopped
5 garlic cloves, chopped
1 lb/450 g ripe tomatoes
2 tortillas, preferably stale,
 cut into small pieces
pinch of ground cloves
pinch of fennel seeds
⅛ tsp each ground cinnamon,
 coriander, and cumin
3 tbsp lightly toasted sesame
 seeds or sesame seed paste
3 tbsp slivered or coarsely
 ground blanched almonds
2 tbsp raisins
1 tbsp peanut butter (optional)
2 cups chicken stock
3–4 tbsp grated semisweet
 chocolate, plus extra
 to garnish
2 tsp mild chili powder,
 such as ancho or New Mexico
3 tbsp vegetable oil, for cooking
about 1 tbsp lime juice
salt and pepper

This great Mexican celebration dish, ladled out at village fiestas, birthday parties, baptisms, and weddings, is known for its unusual, but tasty combination of chilies and chocolate.

1 Using metal tongs, roast each chili over an open flame for a few seconds until the color darkens on all sides. Alternatively, roast in an unoiled skillet over medium heat for 30 seconds, turning constantly.

2 Place the roasted chilies in a heatproof bowl or a pan and pour over enough boiling water to cover. Cover with a lid and let soften for at least 1 hour or overnight. Once or twice, lift the lid and rearrange the chilies so that they soak evenly.

3 Remove the softened chilies with a slotted spoon. Discard the stems and seeds and cut the flesh into pieces. Place in a food processor or blender.

4 Add the onion, garlic, tomatoes, tortillas, cloves, fennel seeds, cinnamon, coriander, cumin, sesame seeds, almonds, raisins, and peanut butter, if using, then process to combine. With the motor running, add enough stock through the feeder tube to make a smooth paste. Stir in the remaining stock, plus the chocolate and chili powder.

5 Heat the oil in a heavy-bottom pan until it is smoking, then pour in the mole mixture. It will splatter and pop as it hits the hot oil. Cook for 10 minutes, stirring occasionally to prevent it burning. Season to taste with salt, pepper, and lime juice, garnish with a little grated chocolate, and serve.

Cilantro Mayonnaise

Making your own mayonnaise is very straightforward, especially with a food processor or blender. The addition of a green chili gives it that traditional Mexican flavor.

 prepare 10 minutes,
plus 30 minutes' chilling
cook no cooking required
serves 4

1 egg
2 tsp prepared mustard
½ tsp salt
squeeze of lemon juice
2 tbsp chopped fresh cilantro
1 fresh mild green chili,
 such as poblano, seeded
 and very finely chopped
1¼ cups olive oil

1 Place the egg in a food processor or blender, add the mustard and salt, and process for 30 seconds.

2 Add the lemon juice, chopped cilantro, and chili and process briefly.

3 With the motor still running, add the olive oil through the feeder tube in a thin, steady stream. The mixture will thicken after half the oil has been added.

4 Continue adding the remaining oil until it is all absorbed. Transfer to a serving bowl, cover, and let chill in the refrigerator for 30 minutes to allow the flavors to develop before serving.

Note Recipes using raw eggs should be avoided by infants, the elderly, pregnant women, convalescents, and anyone suffering from an illness.

Potatoes with Chipotle Cream

prepare 10 minutes

cook 45 minutes

serves 4

2 lb 12 oz/1.25 kg baking
  potatoes, peeled and
  cut into chunks
pinch of salt
pinch of sugar
scant 1 cup sour cream
½ cup vegetable or
  chicken stock
3 garlic cloves,
  very finely chopped
few shakes of bottled
  chipotle salsa
8 oz/225 g goat cheese, sliced
6 oz/175 g mozzarella or
  Cheddar cheese, grated
1¾ oz/50 g Parmesan or
  Romano cheese, grated

This makes a luscious side dish to serve with meat, or a satisfying vegetarian main course. Goat cheese is a traditional food of Mexico, and is enjoying great renewed popularity.

1 Preheat the oven to 350°F/180°C. Place the potatoes in a pan of water with the salt and sugar. Bring to a boil and cook for 10 minutes, or until they are half cooked.

2 Combine the sour cream with the stock, garlic, and the chipotle salsa in a bowl.

3 Arrange half the potatoes in an ovenproof casserole. Pour half the sour cream sauce over the potatoes and cover with the goat cheese slices. Top with the remaining potatoes and the sauce.

4 Sprinkle with the grated mozzarella cheese, then with the grated Parmesan cheese.

5 Bake in the oven for 30 minutes, or until the potatoes are tender and the cheese topping is lightly golden and crisp in places. Serve immediately.

Squash with Chilies & Corn

prepare 10 minutes

cook 10 minutes

serves 4–6

2 ears of corn

2 small zucchini or other
 green summer squash, such
 as pattypans, cubed or sliced

2 small yellow summer squash,
 cubed or sliced

2 tbsp butter, for cooking

3 garlic cloves,
 very finely chopped

3–4 large, ripe, flavorful
 tomatoes, diced

several pinches of mild chili
 powder, such as ancho or
 New Mexico

several pinches of ground cumin

½ fresh green chili, such as
 jalapeño or serrano, seeded
 and chopped

pinch of sugar

salt and pepper

Garlicky butter and a hint of chili flavor this summertime vegetable pot of squash and corn. Serve alongside almost any meaty main course; good, too, with fajitas.

1 Bring about 2 inches/5 cm of water to a boil in the bottom of a steamer. Add the corn, zucchini, and summer squash to the top part of the steamer, cover, and let steam for about 3 minutes, depending on their maturity and freshness. Alternatively, blanch in a pan of boiling salted water for 3 minutes, then drain. Set aside until cool enough to handle.

2 Using a large knife, slice the kernels off the cobs and set aside.

3 Melt the butter in a heavy-bottom skillet. Add the garlic and cook for 1 minute to soften. Add the tomatoes, chili powder, cumin, chili, and sugar. Season to taste with salt and pepper and cook for a few minutes, or until the flavors have mingled.

4 Add the corn, zucchini, and squash. Cook for 2 minutes, stirring, to warm through. Serve immediately.

Potatoes in Tomatillo Sauce

Earthy potatoes, served in a tangy spicy tomatillo sauce and topped with scallions and sour cream, are delicious either as a side dish with simmered or braised meat, or as a vegetarian main course.

prepare 5 minutes
cook 25 minutes
serves 6

1 Place the potatoes in a pan of salted water. Bring to a boil and cook for 15 minutes, or until almost tender. Do not overcook them. Drain and set aside.

2 Lightly char the onion, garlic, chili, and tomatillos in a heavy-bottom unoiled skillet. Set aside. When cool enough to handle, peel and chop the onion, garlic, and chili; chop the tomatillos or tomatoes. Place in a food processor or blender with half the stock and process to form a purée. Add the cumin, thyme, and oregano and stir well to combine.

3 Heat the oil in the heavy-bottom skillet. Add the purée and cook for 5 minutes, stirring, to reduce slightly and concentrate the flavors.

4 Add the potatoes and zucchini to the purée and pour in the rest of the stock. Add about half the cilantro and cook for an additional 5 minutes, or until the zucchini are tender.

5 Transfer to a serving bowl and serve sprinkled with the remaining chopped cilantro to garnish.

2 lb 4 oz/1 kg small waxy potatoes, peeled
1 onion, halved and unpeeled
8 garlic cloves, unpeeled
1 fresh green chili, such as jalapeño or serrano
8 tomatillos, outer husks removed, or small tart tomatoes
1 cup chicken, meat, or vegetable stock, preferably homemade
½ tsp ground cumin
1 fresh thyme sprig or generous pinch of dried thyme
1 fresh oregano sprig or generous pinch of dried oregano
2 tbsp vegetable or virgin olive oil
1 zucchini, coarsely chopped
1 bunch fresh cilantro, chopped

Zucchini & Summer Squash with Chorizo

prepare 10 minutes

cook 10 minutes

serves 4

2 zucchini, thinly sliced

2 yellow summer squash,
  thinly sliced

2 chorizo sausages,
  diced or sliced

3 garlic cloves,
  very finely chopped

juice of ½–1 lime

salt and pepper

1–2 tbsp chopped fresh cilantro,
  to serve

**The spicy richness of chorizo marries well
with zucchini and squash, giving them a real
flavor lift.**

1 Cook the zucchini and summer squash in a pan of boiling salted water for 3–4 minutes, or until they are just tender. Drain well.

2 Brown the chorizo in a heavy-bottom skillet, stirring with a spoon to break up into pieces. Pour off any excess fat from the browned chorizo, then add the garlic and blanched zucchini and summer squash. Cook for a few minutes, stirring gently, to combine the flavors.

3 Stir in the lime juice to taste. Season to taste with salt and pepper and serve immediately, sprinkled with chopped cilantro.

Spicy Fragrant Black Bean Chili

 prepare 15 minutes,
plus 8 hours' soaking

cook 2½–2¾ hours

serves 4

14 oz/400 g dried black beans
2 tbsp olive oil
1 onion, chopped
5 garlic cloves, roughly chopped
2 bacon slices, diced (optional)
½–1 tsp ground cumin
½–1 tsp mild red chili powder,
  such as ancho
1 red bell pepper, diced
1 carrot, diced
14 oz/400 g fresh tomatoes,
  diced, or chopped canned
1 bunch fresh cilantro,
  roughly chopped
salt and pepper

Black beans are fragrant and flavorful; enjoy this chilied bean stew Mexican-style with soft tortillas, or Californian-style in a bowl with crisp tortilla chips crumbled in.

1 Soak the beans overnight, then drain. Place in a pan, cover with water, and bring to a boil. Boil for 10 minutes, then reduce the heat and let simmer for 1½ hours, or until tender. Drain well, reserving 1 cup of the cooking liquid.

2 Heat the oil in a skillet. Add the onion and garlic and cook for 2 minutes, stirring. Add the bacon, if using, and cook, stirring occasionally, until the bacon is cooked and the onion is softened.

3 Stir in the cumin and chili powder and continue to cook for a moment or two. Add the red bell pepper, carrot, and tomatoes. Cook over medium heat for 5 minutes.

4 Add half the chopped cilantro and the beans and their reserved liquid. Season to taste with salt and pepper. Let simmer for 30–45 minutes, or until very flavorful and thickened.

5 Stir in the remaining cilantro, adjust the seasoning, and serve immediately.

Refried Beans

Frijoles refritos, to give them their proper name, are simply a Mexican must, and while you can depend on the canned variety, why not enjoy the real thing now and again?

prepare 10 minutes,
plus 8 hours' soaking
cook 2¼ hours
serves 4

1 Soak the beans overnight, then drain. Place in a large pan with the quartered onion, the herbs, and chili. Pour over enough cold water to cover and bring to a boil. Reduce the heat, cover, and let simmer gently for 2 hours, or until the beans are very tender.

2 Drain the beans, reserving the cooking liquid, and discard the onion, herbs, and chili.

3 Place two-thirds of the beans with the cooking liquid in a food processor or blender and process until coarsely blended.

4 Heat the oil in a heavy-bottom skillet over medium heat. Add the chopped onion and cook for 10 minutes, or until soft and golden. Add the cumin and cook, stirring, for 2 minutes. Stir in the puréed and reserved beans and cook, stirring constantly, until the liquid reduces and the mixture thickens. Stir in the grated cheese, if using, and cook, stirring, until melted. Serve immediately with tortilla chips.

1⅓ cups dried pinto beans
2 onions, 1 quartered and
  1 chopped
1 chopped and 1 whole bay leaf
1 fresh thyme sprig
1 dried red chili, such as ancho
3 tbsp olive oil
2 tsp ground cumin
3 oz/85 g Cheddar cheese,
  grated (optional)
tortilla chips, to serve

Mexican Beans

prepare 15 minutes,
plus 8 hours' soaking

cook 2½ hours

serves 4–6

1 lb 2 oz/500 g dried pinto
  or cranberry beans
1 fresh mint sprig
1 fresh thyme sprig
1 fresh flat-leaf parsley sprig
1 onion, cut into chunks
salt
shredded scallion, to garnish
warmed flour or soft
  corn tortillas, to serve

**A pot of beans, bubbling away on the stove,
is the basic everyday food of Mexico—delicious
and healthy!**

1 Pick through the beans and remove any bits of grit or stones. Cover the beans with cold water and let soak overnight. If you want to cut down on soaking time, bring the beans to a boil in a pan, cook for 5 minutes, then remove from the heat and let stand, covered, for 2 hours.

2 Drain the beans, place in a pan, and cover with fresh water. Add the herb sprigs. Bring to a boil, then reduce the heat to very low and cook gently, covered, for 2 hours, or until the beans are tender. The best way to check that they are done is to sample a bean or two every so often after 1¾ hours' cooking time.

3 Add the onion chunks and continue to cook until the onion and beans are very tender.

4 To serve as a side dish, drain, season to taste with salt, and serve in bowls lined with warmed tortillas, garnished with shredded scallion.

Rice with Lime

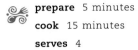

prepare 5 minutes

cook 15 minutes

serves 4

2 tbsp vegetable oil
1 small onion,
  very finely chopped
3 garlic cloves,
  very finely chopped
scant 1 cup long-grain rice
2 cups chicken or
  vegetable stock
juice of 1 lime
1 tbsp chopped fresh cilantro
lime zest, to garnish
lime wedges, to serve (optional)

The tangy citrus taste of lime is marvelous with all sorts of rice dishes. Although not typically Mexican, you could add wild rice to this dish, if liked.

1 Heat the oil in an ovenproof casserole or heavy-bottom pan. Add the onion and garlic and cook gently, stirring occasionally, for 2 minutes. Add the rice and cook for an additional 1 minute, stirring. Pour in the stock, increase the heat, and bring the rice to a boil. Reduce the heat to a very low simmer.

2 Cover and cook the rice for 10 minutes, or until the rice is just tender and the liquid is absorbed.

3 Sprinkle in the lime juice and fork the rice to fluff up and to mix in the juice. Sprinkle with the chopped cilantro, then garnish with lime zest and serve with lime wedges, if wished.

Spicy Rice

Both full of color and flavor, this is so much more inviting than plain boiled rice. Add some canned red kidney beans or black-eyed peas with the stock for a more substantial and tasty alternative.

 prepare 15 minutes, plus 5 minutes' standing
cook 30 minutes
serves 4

1 Heat the oil in a large, heavy-bottom pan over medium heat. Add the scallions, celery, and garlic and cook for 5 minutes, or until softened. Add the bell peppers, corn, and chilies and cook for 5 minutes.

2 Add the rice and cumin and cook, stirring to coat the grains in the oil, for 2 minutes.

3 Stir in the stock and half the chopped cilantro and bring to a boil. Reduce the heat, cover, and let simmer for 15 minutes, or until nearly all the liquid has been absorbed and the rice is just tender.

4 Remove from the heat and fluff up with a fork. Stir in the remaining chopped cilantro and season to taste with salt and pepper. Let stand, covered, for 5 minutes before serving. Serve garnished with cilantro sprigs.

3 tbsp olive oil
6 scallions, chopped
1 celery stalk,
  very finely chopped
3 garlic cloves,
  very finely chopped
2 green bell peppers,
  seeded and chopped
corn kernels,
  cut from 1 corn cob
2 fresh mild green chilies,
  such as poblano, seeded
  and very finely chopped
generous 1¼ cups
  long-grain rice
2 tsp ground cumin
2½ cups chicken or
  vegetable stock
2 tbsp chopped fresh cilantro
salt and pepper
fresh cilantro sprigs, to garnish

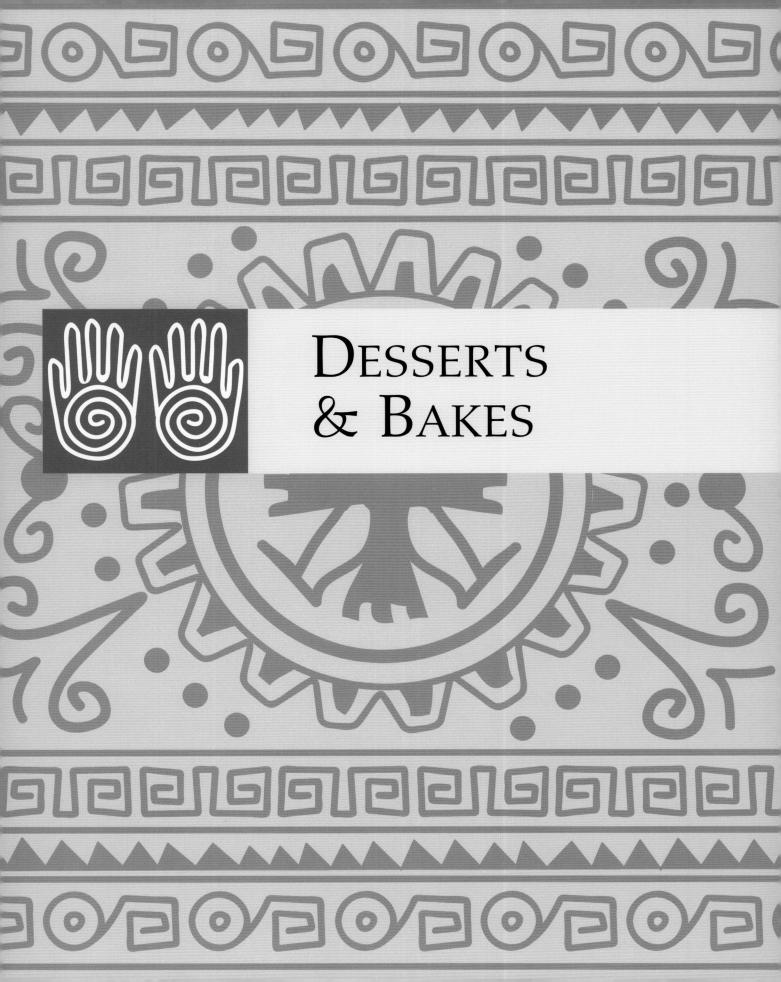

DESSERTS & BAKES

Chocolate Chip & Chili Ice Cream

prepare 15–25 minutes,
plus 15 minutes'–2 hours'
processing or freezing,
and 15 minutes' softening
cook 10 minutes
serves 4

1 egg
1 egg yolk
generous ¼ cup superfine sugar
5½ oz/150 g semisweet
  chocolate, finely chopped
scant 2½ cups milk
1 dried red chili, such as ancho
1 vanilla bean
scant 2½ cups heavy cream
5½ oz/150 g semisweet, milk,
  or white chocolate chips

Chocolate and chili are a classic Mexican combination with savory dishes, but can also be used together in sweet dishes. The chili just gives a warmth and richness to the chocolate.

1 Place the egg, egg yolk, and sugar in a heatproof bowl set over a pan of simmering water. Beat until light and fluffy.

2 Place the chopped chocolate, milk, chili, and vanilla bean in a separate pan and heat gently until the chocolate has dissolved and the milk is almost boiling. Pour onto the egg mixture, discarding the chili and vanilla bean, and beat well. Let cool.

3 Lightly whip the cream in a separate bowl. Fold into the cold mixture with the chocolate chips. Transfer to an ice-cream machine and process for 15 minutes, or according to the manufacturer's instructions. Alternatively, transfer to a freezerproof container and freeze for 1 hour, or until partially frozen. Remove from the freezer, transfer to a bowl, and beat to break down the ice crystals. Freeze again for 30 minutes, then beat again. Freeze once more until firm.

4 Transfer the ice cream to the refrigerator 15 minutes before serving. Serve in scoops.

Note Recipes using raw eggs should be avoided by infants, the elderly, pregnant women, convalescents, and anyone suffering from an illness.

Mexican Cooler

 prepare 15 minutes,
plus 2 hours' freezing
cook no cooking required
serves 4

1 pineapple
1 large piece watermelon
generous 1½ cups strawberries
 or other berries
1 mango, peach, or nectarine
1 banana, sliced
orange juice
superfine sugar, to taste

Keep a store of prepared fruit in the freezer, then whirl it up into this refreshing dessert, which is as light and healthy as it is satisfying. You can vary the fruit as you like.

1 Cover 2 baking sheets with sheets of plastic wrap.

2 Peel and slice the pineapple, then remove the core and cut the flesh into pieces. Peel and seed the watermelon, then cut into small pieces. Hull the strawberries, then slice or leave whole. Slice the mango lengthwise on either side of the flat central seed. Peel the 2 mango pieces and dice the flesh. Slice and peel any remaining flesh around the seed, then dice. Peel the banana and slice.

3 Arrange all of the fruit on top of the sheets and open freeze for at least 2 hours, or until firm and icy.

4 Place one type of fruit in a food processor and process until it is all broken up into small pieces.

5 Add a little orange juice and sugar, to taste, and continue to process until it forms a granular mixture. Repeat with the remaining fruit. Arrange in chilled bowls and serve immediately.

Guava, Lime, & Tequila Sherbet

When you want to chill out, literally, this ice-cold dessert will hit the spot. It couldn't be more elegant. To add a finishing touch, decorate with lime slices or twists or finely pared strips of rind.

 prepare 20 minutes, plus 2½ hours' chilling and 15 minutes' thawing
cook 10 minutes
serves 4

scant 1 cup superfine sugar
scant 2 cups water
4 fresh ripe guavas or
  8 canned guava halves
2 tbsp tequila
juice of ½ lime, or to taste
1 egg white

1 Heat the sugar and water in a heavy-bottom pan over low heat until the sugar has dissolved. When the liquid turns clear, boil for 5 minutes, or until a thick syrup forms. Remove the pan from the heat and let cool.

2 Cut the fresh guavas in half. Scoop out the flesh. Discard the seeds from the fresh or canned guava flesh. Transfer to a food processor or blender and process until smooth.

3 Add the purée to the syrup with the tequila and lime juice. Transfer the mixture to a freezerproof container and freeze for 1 hour, or until slushy.

4 Remove from the freezer and process again until smooth. Return to the freezer and freeze until firm. Process again until smooth. With the motor still running, add the egg white through the feeder tube. Return to the freezer and freeze until solid.

5 Transfer the sherbet to the refrigerator 15 minutes before serving. Serve in scoops.

Note Recipes using raw eggs should be avoided by infants, the elderly, pregnant women, convalescents, and anyone suffering from an illness.

Mexican Flan

🌀 **prepare** 15 minutes,
plus 24 hours' chilling

cook 1½–1¾ hours

serves 4–6

butter, for greasing
1 cup plus 2 tbsp
    superfine sugar
4 tbsp water
a few drops lemon juice
scant 2½ cups milk
1 vanilla bean
2 large eggs
2 large egg yolks

TO DECORATE
sugared fruit
fresh mint sprigs

The contrasting textures and flavors of this creamy dessert with its caramelized topping make it popular with adults and kids alike.

1 Preheat the oven to 325°F/160°C. Lightly grease the side of a 5-cup soufflé dish.

2 To make the caramel, place generous ⅜ cup of the sugar with the water in a pan over medium heat. Cook, stirring, until the sugar dissolves, then boil until golden brown. Remove from the heat and add the lemon juice. Pour into the dish and swirl around. Set aside.

3 Pour the milk into a pan. Slit the vanilla bean lengthwise and add it to the milk. Bring to a boil, remove the pan from the heat and stir in the remaining sugar, stirring until it dissolves. Set aside.

4 Beat the eggs and yolks together in a bowl. Pour the milk mixture over them, whisking. Remove the vanilla bean. Strain the egg mixture into a bowl, then transfer to the soufflé dish.

5 Place the dish in a roasting pan with boiling water to come two-thirds up the side. Bake in the preheated oven for 75–90 minutes, or until a knife inserted in the center comes out clean. Let cool completely. Cover with plastic wrap and let chill for at least 24 hours.

6 Run a knife around the edge. Place an upturned serving plate on top of the soufflé dish, then invert the plate and dish, giving a sharp shake. Lift off the dish and serve, decorated with sugared fruit and mint sprigs.

Mexican Bread Pudding

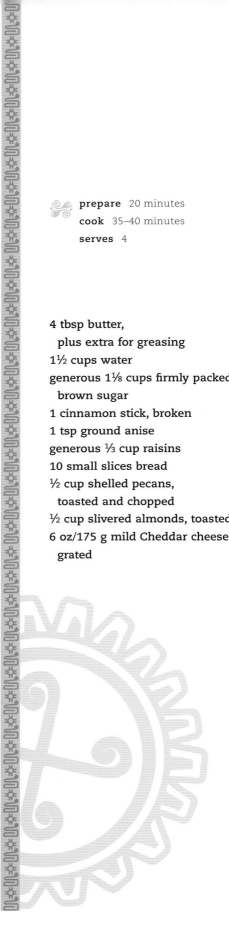

prepare 20 minutes
cook 35–40 minutes
serves 4

4 tbsp butter,
   plus extra for greasing
1½ cups water
generous 1⅛ cups firmly packed
   brown sugar
1 cinnamon stick, broken
1 tsp ground anise
generous ⅓ cup raisins
10 small slices bread
½ cup shelled pecans,
   toasted and chopped
½ cup slivered almonds, toasted
6 oz/175 g mild Cheddar cheese,
   grated

There are many variations of this pudding, called *capirotada*, which turns a loaf of bread into an irresistible dessert. You can use strained cottage cheese in place of the Cheddar for a lighter version.

1 Preheat the oven to 375°F/190°C. Generously grease an ovenproof dish.

2 Heat the water, sugar, cinnamon stick, and anise in a pan over medium heat and stir constantly until the sugar has dissolved. Add the raisins and let simmer for 5 minutes without stirring.

3 Spread butter onto one side of each bread slice and arrange buttered-side up on a baking sheet. Bake in the preheated oven for 5 minutes, or until golden brown. Turn over and bake the other side for 5 minutes.

4 Line the bottom of the ovenproof dish with half the toast. Sprinkle over half the nuts and grated cheese. Remove and discard the cinnamon stick from the raisin mixture, then spoon half of the raisin mixture over the toast. Top with the remaining toast, nuts, grated cheese, and raisin mixture.

5 Bake in the preheated oven for 20–25 minutes, or until set and golden brown on top.

Torta de Cielo

This flat, almond-flavored sponge cake has a dense, moist texture that melts in the mouth. It is the perfect accompaniment to a good strong cup of coffee for either brunch or afternoon tea.

 prepare 15 minutes, plus 30 minutes' cooling
cook 40–50 minutes
serves 4–6

1 cup unsalted butter,
 at room temperature,
 plus extra for greasing
generous 1 cup whole almonds,
 in their skins
generous 1¼ cups sugar
3 eggs, lightly beaten
1 tsp almond extract
1 tsp vanilla extract
9 tbsp all-purpose flour
pinch of salt

TO DECORATE
confectioners' sugar, for dusting
slivered almonds, toasted

1 Preheat the oven to 350°F/180°C. Lightly grease an 8-inch/20-cm round or 7-inch/17.5-cm square cake pan and line the pan with parchment paper.

2 Place the almonds in a food processor and process to form a "mealy" mixture. Set aside.

3 Beat the butter and sugar together in a large bowl until smooth and fluffy. Beat in the eggs, almonds, almond extract, and vanilla extract until well blended.

4 Stir in the flour and salt and mix briefly, until the flour is just incorporated.

5 Pour or spoon the batter into the prepared pan and smooth the surface. Bake in the preheated oven for 40–50 minutes, or until the cake feels spongy when gently pressed.

6 Remove from the oven and let stand on a wire rack to cool. To serve, dust with confectioners' sugar and decorate with toasted slivered almonds.

Peach & Pecan Empanadas

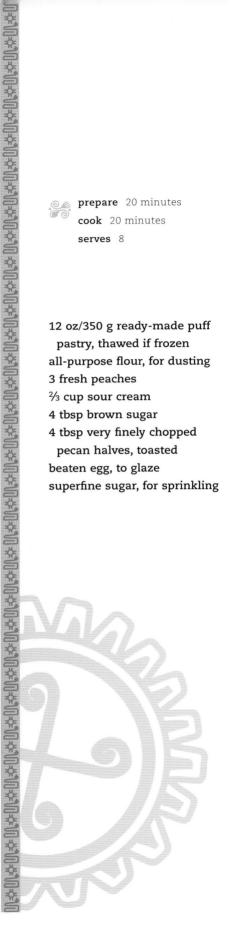

prepare 20 minutes
cook 20 minutes
serves 8

12 oz/350 g ready-made puff
    pastry, thawed if frozen
all-purpose flour, for dusting
3 fresh peaches
⅔ cup sour cream
4 tbsp brown sugar
4 tbsp very finely chopped
    pecan halves, toasted
beaten egg, to glaze
superfine sugar, for sprinkling

Here we have a sweet alternative to savory empanadas, this time with a creamy, fruity filling and a hint of crunchy nut. You could use apricots or mangoes in place of the peaches, if you prefer.

1 Preheat the oven to 400°F/200°C. Roll out the pastry on a lightly floured counter. Using a 6-inch/15-cm saucer as a guide, cut out 8 circles.

2 Place the peaches in a heatproof bowl and pour over enough boiling water to cover. Leave for a few seconds, then drain and peel off the skins. Halve the peaches, remove the pits, and slice the flesh.

3 Place a spoonful of sour cream on one half of each pastry circle and top with a few peach slices. Sprinkle over a little brown sugar and some nuts. Brush all around the edge with a little beaten egg, fold the pastry over the filling, and press the edges together to seal. Crimp the edges with a fork and prick the tops.

4 Place on a baking sheet, brush with beaten egg, and sprinkle with superfine sugar. Bake in the preheated oven for 20 minutes, or until they turn golden brown.

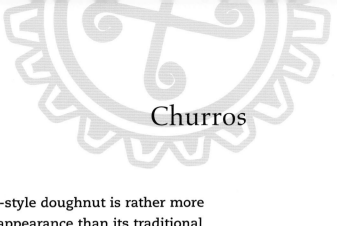

Churros

prepare 25 minutes,
plus 3 minutes' cooling

cook 20 minutes

serves 4

1 cup water

6 tbsp butter or shortening,
    diced

2 tbsp brown sugar

finely grated rind of 1 small
    orange (optional)

pinch of salt

scant 1¼ cups all-purpose flour,
    well sifted

1 tsp ground cinnamon,
    plus extra for dusting

1 tsp vanilla extract

2 eggs

vegetable oil, for deep-frying

superfine sugar, for dusting

This Mexican-style doughnut is rather more appealing in appearance than its traditional relative, since the dough is piped into lengths, which twist into a variety of interesting shapes when deep-fried.

1 Heat the water, butter, brown sugar, orange rind, if using, and salt in a heavy-bottom pan over medium heat until the butter has melted.

2 Add the flour, all at once, the cinnamon and vanilla extract, then remove the pan from the heat and beat rapidly until the mixture pulls away from the side of the pan.

3 Let cool slightly, then beat in the eggs, one at a time, beating well after each addition, until the mixture is thick and smooth. Spoon into a pastry bag fitted with a wide star tip.

4 Heat the oil for deep-frying in a deep-fryer or deep pan to 350–375°F/180–190°C, or until a cube of bread browns in 30 seconds. Pipe 5-inch/13-cm lengths about 3 inches/7.5 cm apart into the oil. Deep-fry for 2 minutes on each side, or until golden brown. Remove with a slotted spoon and drain on paper towels.

5 Dust the churros with superfine sugar and cinnamon and serve.

Empanadas of Banana & Chocolate

Using phyllo pastry makes these empanadas light and crisp on the outside, while the filling of diced banana and pieces of chocolate melt into a scrumptious hot banana-chocolate goo.

 prepare 5 minutes
cook 15 minutes
serves 4–6

1 Preheat the oven to 375°F/190°C. Working one at a time, lay a long rectangular sheet of phyllo pastry out in front of you and brush it with butter.

2 Peel and dice the bananas and place in a bowl. Add the sugar and lemon juice and stir well to combine. Stir in the chocolate.

3 Place a couple of teaspoons of the banana and chocolate mixture in one corner of the pastry, then fold over into a triangle shape to enclose the filling. Continue to fold in a triangular shape, until the phyllo pastry is completely wrapped around the filling.

4 Dust the packages with confectioners' sugar and cinnamon. Place on a baking sheet and continue the process with the remaining phyllo pastry and filling.

5 Bake in the oven for 15 minutes, or until the pastries are golden. Remove from the oven and serve hot—warn people that the filling is very hot.

about 8 sheets of phyllo pastry,
  cut in half lengthwise
melted butter or vegetable oil,
  for brushing
2 ripe sweet bananas
1–2 tsp superfine sugar
juice of ¼ lemon
6–7 oz/175–200 g semisweet
  chocolate, broken into
  small pieces
confectioners' sugar, for dusting
ground cinnamon, for dusting

Bunuelos with Orange-Cinnamon Syrup

prepare 20 minutes,
plus 30 minutes' resting

cook 45 minutes

serves 4

scant 1⅝ cups all-purpose flour,
  plus extra for dusting
1 tsp baking powder
¼ tsp salt
1 tbsp brown sugar
1 egg, beaten
2 tbsp butter, melted
about ½ cup evaporated milk
vegetable oil, for deep-frying

ORANGE-CINNAMON SYRUP
1½ cups water
grated rind of 1 small orange
4 tbsp freshly squeezed
  orange juice
½ cup firmly packed
  brown sugar
1 tbsp honey
2 tsp ground cinnamon

These traditional, plain, sweet fritters are served with their own flavored syrup in which they can be dunked or drenched. Maple syrup, corn syrup, or honey are good alternatives.

1 Sift the flour, baking powder, and salt together into a large bowl. Stir in the sugar. Beat in the egg and butter with enough evaporated milk to form a soft, smooth dough.

2 Shape the dough into 8 balls. Cover and let rest for 30 minutes.

3 Meanwhile, to make the syrup, place the water, orange rind and juice, sugar, honey, and cinnamon in a heavy-bottom pan over medium heat. Bring to a boil, stirring constantly, then reduce the heat and let simmer gently for 20 minutes, or until thickened.

4 Flatten the dough balls to make cakes. Heat the oil for deep-frying in a deep-fryer or deep pan to 350–375°F/ 180–190°C, or until a cube of bread browns in 30 seconds. Deep-fry the bunuelos in batches for 4–5 minutes, turning once, or until golden brown and puffed. Remove with a slotted spoon and drain on paper towels. Serve with the syrup spooned over.

Mexican Wedding Cakes

prepare 25 minutes,
plus 1½ hours' chilling
and cooling
cook 10 minutes
makes about 36

1 cup butter, softened
2 cups confectioners' sugar
1 tsp vanilla extract
scant 1⅝ cups all-purpose flour,
  plus extra for dusting
½ tsp salt
generous ⅝ cup pecan or
  walnut halves, toasted
  and very finely chopped

The name of these traditional Mexican cookies comes from the fact that they look like wedding bells, with their thick white coating of confectioners' sugar. The nut halves can be chopped in a food processor.

1 Cream the butter with half the sugar and the vanilla extract in a large bowl. Sift the flour and salt together into the bowl and fold into the mixture. Stir in the nuts. Cover and let chill in the refrigerator for 1 hour, or until firm.

2 Preheat the oven to 375°F/190°C. With floured hands, shape the dough into 1-inch/2.5-cm balls and place about 1½ inches/4 cm apart on 2 large baking sheets.

3 Bake in the preheated oven for 10 minutes, or until set but not browned, rotating the baking sheets so that the cookies bake evenly. Let cool on the baking sheets for 2–3 minutes.

4 Place the remaining sugar in a shallow dish. Roll the warm cookies in the sugar, then let cool on wire racks for 30 minutes. When cold, roll again in the sugar. Store in airtight containers.

Aztec Oranges

Simplicity itself, this refreshing orange dessert is hard to beat and is the perfect follow-up to a hearty, spiced main course dish.

prepare 15 minutes
cook no cooking required
serves 4–6

1 Using a sharp knife, cut a slice off the top and bottom of the oranges, then remove the peel and pith, cutting downward and taking care to retain the shape of the oranges.

2 Holding the oranges on their side, cut them horizontally into slices.

3 Place the oranges in a nonmetallic bowl. Cut the lime in half and squeeze over the oranges. Sprinkle with the tequila and liqueur, then sprinkle over sugar to taste.

4 Cover and let chill until ready to serve, then transfer to a serving dish and decorate with lime zest.

6 oranges
1 lime
2 tbsp tequila
2 tbsp orange-flavored liqueur
brown sugar, to taste
lime zest, to decorate

Index